KOH SAMUI
TRAVEL GUIDE
2025

**Discover Tropical Paradise Amid
Thailand's Emerald Coast**

Carolyn Marie

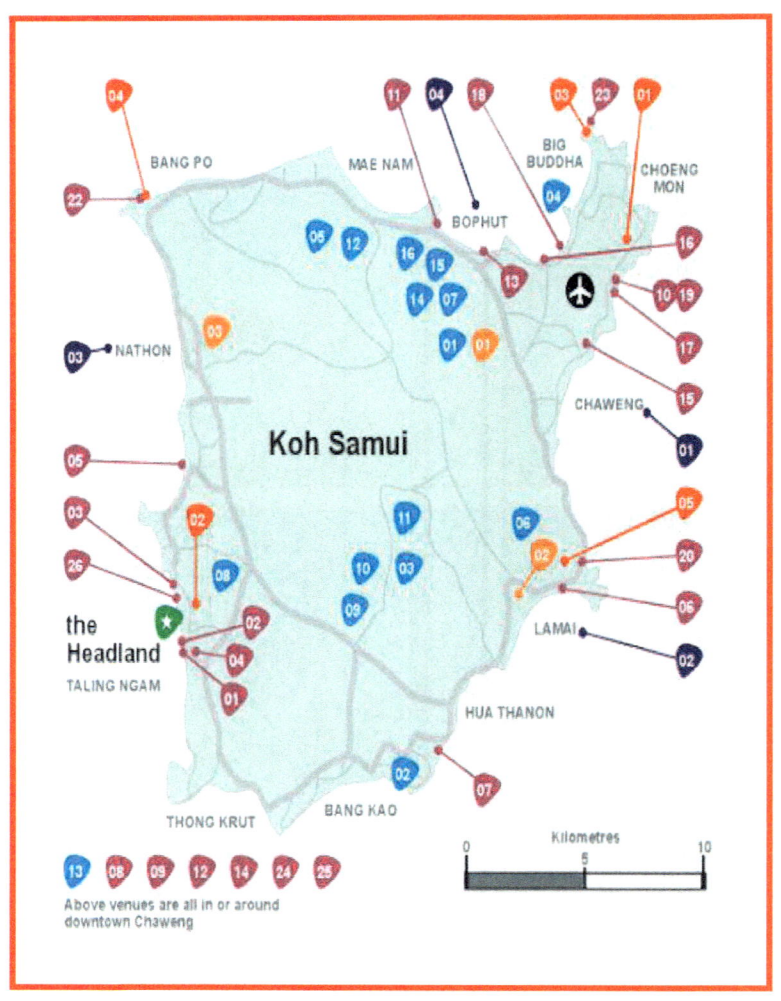

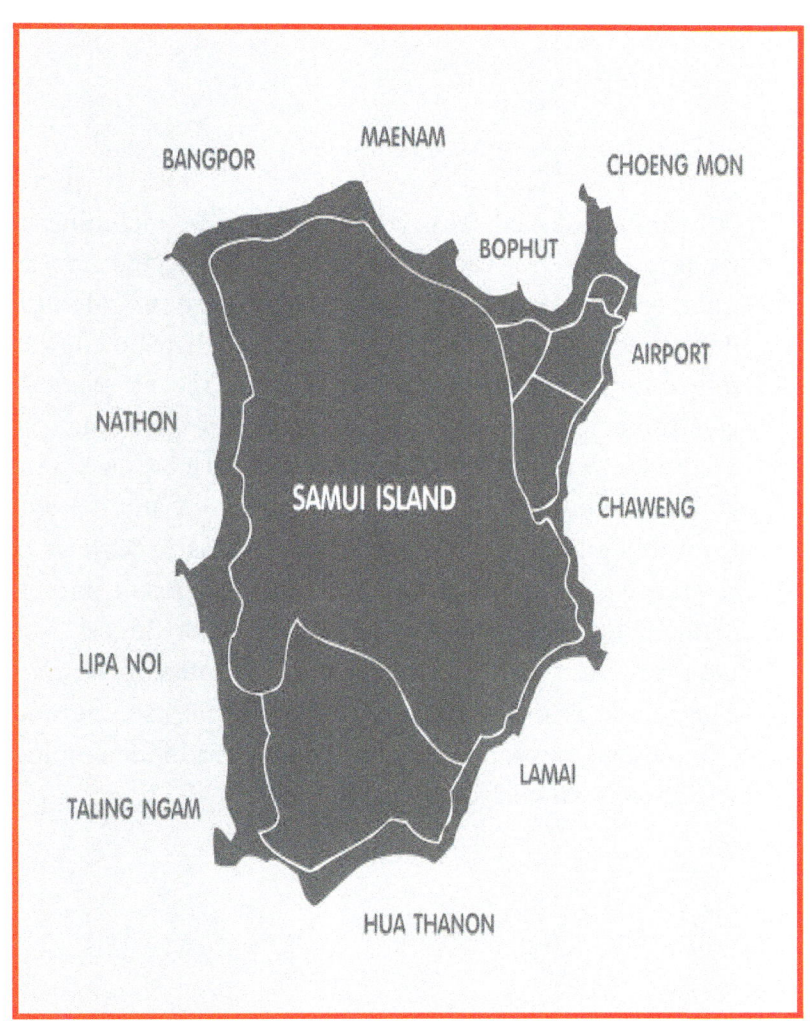

COPYRIGHT © CAROLYN MARIE 2025

All rights reserved. This companion guide, including its content, design, and layout, is protected under international copyright law. No portion of this publication may be reproduced, distributed, or transmitted in any form or by any means whether electronic, mechanical, photocopying, recording, or otherwise without the prior written permission of the author. Unauthorized use or distribution of any material from this guide, including brief quotations in reviews or references, is strictly prohibited and may result in legal action. For permissions, contact the author directly. All inquiries and permissions must be granted in writing. This guide is intended solely for personal use, and any commercial exploitation is expressly forbidden unless specifically authorized by the author.

Disclaimer

This companion guide is provided for informational purposes only. While every effort has been made to ensure accuracy, the author, **CAROLYN MARIE**, and the publisher make no guarantees or warranties about the completeness or reliability of the content. Travel conditions and regulations may change, and it is the reader's responsibility to verify details with relevant authorities. The author is not liable for any errors, omissions, or outcomes resulting from the use of this guide. Readers should use their own judgment and seek professional advice where necessary.

TABLE OF CONTENTS

CHAPTER ONE..**11**
  Introduction to Koh Samui.. 11
    Overview of Koh Samui...................................... 11
    My Personal Experience in Koh Samui.............14
    Why Visit Koh Samui?..22
    A Brief History of Koh Samui............................24
    Geographic Location and Climate......................27
    Best Time to Visit Koh Samui............................ 29
    Essential Travel Information.............................. 31
    Currency and Exchange......................................33
    Language and Local Etiquette............................ 35
    Safety Tips for Tourists......................................37

CHAPTER TWO..**42**
  Beautiful Attractions and Must-Visit Spots.............. 42
    Beaches and Coastal Attractions of Koh Samui 42
    Cultural and Historical Attractions of Koh Samui 50
    Big Buddha Temple (Wat Phra Yai)................... 51
    Wat Plai Laem..53
    Hin Ta and Hin Yai (Grandfather and Grandmother Rocks)..56
    Nature and Adventure in Koh Samui................. 59
    Ang Thong National Marine Park...................... 59

Secret Buddha Garden.. 62
Namuang Waterfalls... 64
Koh Taen (Coral Island)...................................... 66
CHAPTER THREE...69
Hidden Gems and Off-the-Beaten-Path Attractions 69
Lesser-Known Beaches in Koh Samui............... 69
Taling Ngam Beach.. 70
Lipa Noi Beach... 72
Secret Spots for Nature Lovers in Koh Samui.. 75
Overlap Stone... 76
Magic Garden (Tarnim Magic Garden)............. 78
Adventure Opportunities in Koh Samui............ 81
Off-Road Jungle Safari....................................... 82
Zip-lining and Canopy Adventures................... 84
CHAPTER FOUR... 87
Food and Cuisine... 87
Must-Try Local Dishes in Koh Samui............... 87
Best Restaurants in Koh Samui.......................... 91
Fine Dining Options.. 92
Local Street Food and Market Experiences.......94
Vegetarian and Vegan Food Options in Koh Samui... 97
1. The Sanctuary Thailand................................97
2. Luna Lounge..98
3. The Living Room at The Samui Mermaid.....98
4. Samui Institute of Thai Culinary Arts (SITCA) 99

Popular Cafés and Coffee Spots in Koh Samui..... 100

CHAPTER FIVE 104

Accommodation Options on Koh Samui............... 104

Recommended Hotels for Every Budget in Koh Samui.. 104

Luxury Resorts... 104

Mid-Range Hotels...106

Budget-Friendly Options................................. 109

    4. Baan Haad Rin Resort............................110

Unique Stays and Boutique Accommodations in Koh Samui.. 111

CHAPTER SIX.. 117

Getting to Koh Samui.. 117

Airlines Serving Koh Samui............................. 118

Ferry Services.. 120

Transportation Within Koh Samui.................... 122

Public Transportation.......................................123

Renting a Car or Motorbike............................. 124

Driving Tips and Safety Regulations in Koh Samui.. 127

Navigating the Island's Roads.......................... 129

Car Rental Companies and Contact Information in Koh Samui... 131

Popular Car Rental Companies........................132

Directions to Tourist Centers and Attractions. 134

CHAPTER SEVEN 137
Sample Itineraries, Customs, and Traditions 138
Sample Itineraries for Different Types of Travelers in Koh Samui 138
3-Day Itinerary for First-Time Visitors 138
5-Day Adventure Itinerary 140
Relaxation-Focused Itinerary 142
Dos and Don'ts for Respectful Travel in Koh Samui 144
Useful Phrases in Thai 148
Appendix 152
A.1 Emergency Contact Numbers 153
A.2 Bank Locations and ATMs 154
A.3 Recommended Travel Apps for Koh Samui ... 156
A.4 Tourist Information Centers and Contact Details 158

CHAPTER ONE

Introduction to Koh Samui

Overview of Koh Samui

Koh Samui, Thailand's second-largest island, is a tropical paradise located in the Gulf of Thailand. Known for its palm-fringed beaches, lush mountainous rainforests, and vibrant cultural scene, Koh Samui has become a world-renowned travel destination that attracts a diverse range of visitors. From luxury travelers seeking five-star resorts to backpackers exploring the island's hidden corners, Koh Samui offers something for everyone. It has transformed from a quiet, isolated fishing island into a bustling hub for tourism, while still maintaining the natural beauty and charm that originally drew people to its shores.

The island is approximately 228.7 square kilometers, making it large enough to offer a wide variety of experiences, yet small enough for visitors to navigate with ease. Its white-sand beaches and crystal-clear waters are a haven for sun-seekers, while its lush interiors are filled with waterfalls, hiking trails, and hidden cultural gems. The island is also surrounded by smaller, equally stunning islands like Koh Tao and Koh Phangan, making it a perfect base for island-hopping adventures.

Koh Samui's climate is tropical, characterized by warm temperatures year-round and two primary seasons: dry and rainy. The best time to visit is typically between December and March, when the weather is at its most pleasant, with clear skies and cooler breezes. However, the island is also popular during the shoulder seasons (April-June and September-November), when fewer crowds allow for a more relaxed experience.

The island's culture is deeply rooted in Thai traditions, with a strong presence of Buddhist influence seen in its many temples and religious sites, such as the famous Big Buddha and Wat Plai Laem. Koh Samui is also a place where modernity meets tradition—glitzy beach clubs and fine-dining restaurants exist alongside local markets and fishing villages that preserve the island's history and heritage.

For adventure seekers, Koh Samui offers activities like snorkeling, diving, hiking, and zip-lining, as well as trips to the nearby Ang Thong National Marine Park, a stunning archipelago of 42 islands known for its pristine nature and marine life. Nature lovers will find peace in the island's many waterfalls, secret beaches, and hidden jungle retreats, while food lovers can savor the local flavors of southern Thai cuisine, from fresh seafood to spicy curries.

Whether you're looking for luxury, relaxation, adventure, or cultural exploration, Koh Samui offers it all in an idyllic, tropical setting. Its combination of natural beauty, rich culture, and modern conveniences makes it one of Thailand's most beloved travel destinations, offering an unforgettable experience for every type of traveler.

My Personal Experience in Koh Samui

The moment I stepped off the plane at Koh Samui's charming little airport, I felt the air change. It was warm but gentle, carrying the scent of saltwater and tropical flowers, as if the island itself was welcoming me. The airport felt more like a tropical resort, with its open-air terminal and lush gardens. I couldn't help but smile; it felt like I had landed in paradise.

After grabbing my bags, I hopped into a taxi toward Chaweng Beach, one of the island's most famous stretches of sand. As we drove through winding roads, glimpses of the turquoise sea flashed through the palm trees, each view more stunning than the last. I'd read about Koh Samui's beauty, but seeing it in person was something entirely different. The island was alive—vibrant colors, bustling markets, and an energy that seemed to hum in the air.

When I reached my hotel, a boutique resort nestled along the shoreline, the first thing I did was head to the beach. I kicked off my sandals, feeling the soft, powdery sand between my toes as I walked toward the water. It was quiet, despite being a popular area, with the gentle lapping of the waves offering a peaceful rhythm. I sat on a sun lounger, watching as the sky began to change hues—the blues deepened into oranges and pinks, painting the horizon in a way that only a tropical sunset can.

The next day, I rented a motorbike to explore the island. I rode through sleepy villages where locals sat outside small shops, chatting and laughing. It was a different side of Koh Samui, far from the busy tourist areas, and it made me appreciate the island even more. I made my way to Wat Phra Yai, the famous Big Buddha statue that stands majestically on a small islet connected by a causeway. Standing at the foot of the towering Buddha, looking out over the sparkling sea, I felt a deep sense of calm wash over me. The hum of visitors and the tinkling of prayer bells created an almost meditative atmosphere.

One of the highlights of my trip was the day I ventured into the heart of Koh Samui's jungle. I had heard whispers about a hidden waterfall deep within the island, and my adventurous side couldn't resist. Armed with a map, I trekked through the dense greenery, the path winding through towering trees and over moss-covered rocks. The sounds of the jungle chirping birds, rustling leaves, and distant insect calls added a magical layer to the experience. When I finally arrived at Namuang Waterfall, it felt like I had discovered something secret. Water cascaded down the rocks into a crystal-clear pool, and I immediately jumped in, the cool water a refreshing contrast to the sticky jungle heat. I floated there for what felt like hours, staring up at the canopy above, feeling completely at peace.

In the evenings, I explored Fisherman's Village in Bophut, a charming area filled with beachfront restaurants, quaint shops, and street food stalls. The scent of grilled seafood filled the air, and I couldn't resist trying a dish of fresh prawns seasoned with lemongrass and lime. The flavors were bright and bold, perfectly capturing the essence of Thai cuisine. I wandered through the night market, picking up handmade souvenirs and chatting with the friendly locals. There was a sense of warmth and community that was infectious. It made me feel like I belonged, even if only for a short time.

One night, I attended a traditional Thai cooking class tucked away in a family-run establishment. I learned how to make Pad Thai and Tom Kha Gai, guided by an elderly woman who treated cooking like an art form. The process was rhythmic and almost meditative, the aroma of coconut milk and spices filling the air as we cooked together. That evening, sharing the meal I had prepared with new friends from the class, I felt connected not just to the people, but to the island itself.

As my trip came to an end, I found myself sitting on the balcony of my hotel, gazing out at the sea. Koh Samui had shown me so many sides of itself: its wild beauty, its vibrant culture, and its gentle, peaceful spirit. It was an island of contrasts, where luxury resorts met untamed jungle, where bustling markets stood beside serene temples. And yet, it all came together in a way that made perfect sense.

Koh Samui wasn't just a place I had visited; it was a place I had experienced with all my senses. The memories of its sunsets, its food, its people, and its incredible landscapes stayed with me long after I left. I knew, as I boarded my flight home, that I would return someday. Koh Samui had left an imprint on me one that would call me back to its shores, again and again.

Why Visit Koh Samui?

Koh Samui is a tropical paradise that offers an ideal balance of natural beauty, cultural richness, and modern amenities, making it a must-visit destination for all types of travelers. Whether you're seeking a relaxing beach holiday, a cultural exploration, or an adventure-filled journey, Koh Samui delivers on every front. Its pristine white-sand beaches, crystal-clear waters, and luxurious resorts provide the perfect backdrop for relaxation, while its vibrant nightlife, diverse dining options, and lively markets ensure that there is always something to see and do.

One of the island's greatest attractions is its diversity of experiences. You can spend your days lounging on world-famous beaches like Chaweng and Lamai or venture into the jungle to discover waterfalls, hidden gardens, and breathtaking viewpoints. Koh Samui's coastal waters offer an abundance of marine life, making it a popular destination for snorkeling, diving, and boating enthusiasts. The nearby Ang Thong National Marine Park, with its unspoiled islands and azure lagoons, is an incredible place for day trips.

For those interested in culture, Koh Samui is home to iconic religious landmarks like the Big Buddha and Wat Plai Laem. The island's many temples reflect Thailand's deep-rooted Buddhist heritage, providing a peaceful contrast to the more touristy areas. Traditional festivals, such as Songkran (the Thai New Year), bring visitors even closer to the island's unique customs and traditions.

Koh Samui is also famous for its wellness and spa retreats, attracting visitors looking for rejuvenation through yoga, meditation, and holistic therapies. The island's local cuisine, from fresh seafood to southern Thai dishes, ensures that food lovers are in for a treat. Whether you're indulging in street food at the night markets or enjoying a fine dining experience by the sea, the flavors of Koh Samui are unforgettable.

Ultimately, Koh Samui's combination of natural beauty, cultural significance, adventure, and leisure make it a perfect destination for anyone looking to escape the ordinary and experience a slice of paradise.

A Brief History of Koh Samui

Koh Samui has a history that dates back over 1,500 years, though its relatively isolated location in the Gulf of Thailand meant that it remained largely untouched by external influences for much of its past. The island was originally inhabited by Malay and Chinese sea traders and fishermen, and early settlers relied on the island's abundant natural resources for survival. In fact, the name "Samui" is believed to have come from the Chinese word "saboey," which means "safe haven," referring to the island's use as a stopover for traders seeking shelter.

For centuries, Koh Samui remained a sleepy, self-sustained island with little connection to the outside world. The island's dense, mountainous interior made it difficult to access, and there were no roads until the 1970s. Instead, locals lived in small fishing villages along the coast, cultivating coconut trees, fishing, and farming to sustain their livelihoods. Coconut plantations were the island's primary industry, and Koh Samui became one of Thailand's leading coconut producers, shipping thousands of coconuts each month to the mainland.

It wasn't until the 1970s that Koh Samui began to gain attention from travelers. The island was discovered by backpackers and adventure seekers who were drawn to its unspoiled beaches and tranquil atmosphere. In 1967, the first foreign visitors arrived by boat, and word of the island's beauty quickly spread. As tourism grew, so did the island's infrastructure. The construction of an airport in the 1980s made Koh Samui more accessible, and the island rapidly developed into a major tourist destination.

Despite its modernization, Koh Samui has retained much of its traditional charm. The local population, originally a mix of Buddhist Thais and Muslim fishermen, has integrated tourism into their daily lives without losing their connection to the land and the sea. Coconut farming continues to be a staple industry, and you can still see trucks filled with coconuts traveling along the island's roads.

Koh Samui's history of isolation, followed by its transformation into a global tourist hotspot, makes it a fascinating destination. While it now boasts world-class resorts, restaurants, and nightlife, it remains rooted in its history as a peaceful, self-reliant island—a place where ancient temples stand side by side with modern beach clubs, and where visitors can still experience the authentic culture and traditions that have shaped this unique island for centuries.

Geographic Location and Climate

Koh Samui is located in the Gulf of Thailand, off the east coast of the Kra Isthmus, which connects the Malay Peninsula with mainland Thailand. As part of the Surat Thani province, Koh Samui sits approximately 700 kilometers south of Bangkok and about 80 kilometers from the eastern coastline of the mainland. The island is part of an archipelago that includes other famous islands like Koh Phangan and Koh Tao, making it an ideal base for island-hopping adventures in the region.

Koh Samui is roughly circular in shape, with a diameter of about 25 kilometers and a total area of 228.7 square kilometers, making it Thailand's second-largest island after Phuket. The island's terrain is a mix of white-sand beaches, palm-fringed coastlines, and a mountainous interior covered in dense rainforest. Its highest point is Khao Pom, a 635-meter-high mountain that dominates the central part of the island, offering panoramic views of the surrounding landscape. While the coastal areas are more developed with resorts, restaurants, and villages, the heart of Koh Samui remains largely untouched and filled with lush jungle and waterfalls.

The island enjoys a tropical monsoon climate, which means it experiences warm temperatures throughout the year with high humidity. However, unlike many other parts of Thailand, Koh Samui has a distinct climate pattern that doesn't follow the usual wet and dry seasons. Instead, it has three main weather periods: dry, hot, and rainy.

The dry season generally runs from December to March, when temperatures are more moderate, and the skies are mostly clear. The hot season follows from April to June, with temperatures reaching their peak, and while it can be warm, it's still a good time for beachgoers. The rainy season, influenced by the northeast monsoon, typically occurs from September to November, bringing heavy, short bursts of rain. However, even during the rainy season, downpours are often followed by sunny intervals, so it doesn't necessarily detract from the experience.

Because Koh Samui is located in the Gulf of Thailand, it is somewhat sheltered from the more extreme monsoon weather that affects other parts of the country. This makes it a popular year-round destination, although visitors should plan based on their preferences for weather and activities.

Best Time to Visit Koh Samui

The best time to visit Koh Samui is during the dry season, from December to March, when the weather is at its most pleasant. During this period, temperatures range from the mid-20s to low 30s Celsius (77 to 86°F), with low humidity and very little rain. The clear skies and gentle breezes make it the perfect time for beach lovers, and it's also ideal for outdoor activities such as snorkeling, diving, and exploring the island's many natural attractions.

This period is also Koh Samui's peak tourist season, meaning that hotels, restaurants, and attractions are at their busiest. While the island never feels overly crowded due to its size, it's wise to book accommodation and activities in advance if you're visiting during these months.

The shoulder seasons—April to June and September to November—are also great times to visit Koh Samui, depending on your travel preferences. April to June brings warmer temperatures, with highs reaching 35°C (95°F), which is perfect for those who enjoy hot, sunny weather. These months also coincide with Thailand's Songkran Festival (Thai New Year) in April, an exciting time to experience the island's cultural festivities. The crowds tend to thin out after March, making it an appealing time for travelers who prefer fewer tourists but still want mostly good weather.

The rainy season, from September to November, is considered the low season for tourism. During this time, Koh Samui experiences more frequent rain showers, although they are often short-lived and followed by clear skies. If you're looking for a quieter, more budget-friendly experience, this is an excellent time to visit. Hotels and resorts often offer lower rates, and the island feels more peaceful. However, certain water-based activities like diving and snorkeling may be limited due to choppier seas during the monsoon.

In summary, the ideal time to visit Koh Samui depends on what you seek from your trip. For perfect beach weather and vibrant island life, December to March is the top choice. For those who enjoy hotter temperatures or want to experience the island with fewer crowds, the shoulder seasons are an excellent option. Even the rainy season offers its own charms, with fewer tourists, discounted rates, and occasional sunny spells.

Essential Travel Information

Koh Samui, as one of Thailand's most popular tourist destinations, is well-equipped to cater to international travelers, but having a solid understanding of the essential travel information can make your visit smoother and more enjoyable. From practical tips on currency exchange to understanding local etiquette and safety advice, this section covers all the basics you'll need to navigate the island with ease and confidence.

Koh Samui's main points of entry for tourists are the Samui International Airport, which serves both domestic and international flights, and the ferry ports that connect the island with the mainland. While the island is relatively small, getting around efficiently and knowing where to access essential services like banks, health care, and transportation is key to having a worry-free stay. Whether you're traveling for a quick beach getaway or an extended stay, knowing these essential details will ensure a hassle-free experience.

Currency and Exchange

The official currency of Thailand is the Thai Baht (THB), and it is the only currency accepted for everyday transactions on Koh Samui. As of recent exchange rates, one US dollar is equivalent to approximately 30-35 THB, though this can fluctuate. It's always a good idea to check the current exchange rates before your trip.

Currency exchange is widely available on Koh Samui, and you'll find a variety of options, from dedicated exchange booths to banks. Exchange booths are commonly located in tourist areas, including Chaweng Beach, Lamai Beach, and around the main ferry terminals. They tend to offer competitive rates, but it's always a good idea to compare rates between multiple booths to ensure you're getting the best deal. Banks offer slightly more secure exchanges but may have slightly lower rates and longer processing times.

ATMs are also available throughout Koh Samui, particularly in the more populated areas. Most ATMs accept international credit and debit cards, making it convenient to withdraw Thai Baht directly. However, be mindful of transaction fees, both from your home bank and the local ATM, which can add up. It's often more cost-effective to withdraw larger sums at once rather than multiple smaller transactions.

Credit and debit cards are widely accepted in hotels, restaurants, and larger stores, but many smaller establishments and street vendors operate on a cash-only basis. Always carry some cash with you for small purchases, local markets, or transportation. It's also worth noting that when using foreign cards in Thailand, some vendors may apply a small surcharge to the bill, particularly for transactions involving cards issued outside of Thailand.

Tipping is not customary in Thailand, but it is appreciated for good service. In tourist areas like Koh Samui, a small tip (around 10% of the bill) is often expected at restaurants. For services such as taxi rides or massages, a small tip is also appreciated.

Language and Local Etiquette

The official language of Thailand is Thai, and it is the primary language spoken on Koh Samui. In most tourist areas, however, English is widely understood, especially in hotels, restaurants, and tour operators. Many local vendors, shopkeepers, and taxi drivers also have a basic understanding of English, but knowing a few key Thai phrases can go a long way in making your trip smoother and more enjoyable. Simple greetings like "Sawadee" (hello), "Khob khun" (thank you), and "Tao rai?" (how much?) are always appreciated by locals and can help foster positive interactions.

When it comes to local etiquette, understanding and respecting Thai customs is important for ensuring a warm and welcoming reception during your stay. Thai culture places a strong emphasis on respect, politeness, and avoiding confrontation, and these values extend into daily interactions.

A key element of Thai etiquette is the traditional greeting, known as the "wai," which involves placing your hands together in a prayer-like gesture and bowing slightly. This gesture is used to show respect, particularly when greeting elders or individuals in positions of authority. While foreigners are not expected to initiate the "wai," it is polite to return the gesture when greeted in this manner.

Dress modestly, especially when visiting religious sites like temples. While it's common to wear swimwear on the beach, covering up with a sarong or light clothing is appreciated when walking in public spaces or dining at restaurants. Always remove your shoes when entering a temple or someone's home. It's also considered disrespectful to point your feet at people or religious objects, and touching someone on the head is seen as inappropriate in Thai culture.

Public displays of affection, such as kissing or hugging, are generally frowned upon in Thai society, though holding hands is acceptable. Additionally, avoid raising your voice or displaying anger in public, as this is considered bad form and could lead to an awkward situation.

When visiting temples, always show respect by refraining from loud behavior and inappropriate dress. Women should avoid touching monks or handing objects directly to them. It's also polite to leave a small donation when visiting temples, as they rely on these contributions for maintenance and upkeep.

Safety Tips for Tourists

While Koh Samui is generally considered a safe destination for tourists, it's always important to take basic precautions to ensure a trouble-free trip. Being mindful of personal safety, local laws, and common travel risks will allow you to fully enjoy your time on the island without any unwanted incidents. The following broad and comprehensive safety tips will help you navigate Koh Samui safely and responsibly.

1. Personal Safety
Koh Samui has a low crime rate, but petty theft can occur, particularly in crowded areas like markets or busy beaches. Always keep your belongings secure and be cautious of your surroundings, especially in tourist-heavy areas. Avoid leaving valuables unattended on the beach or in open-view in vehicles. Consider using a money belt or secure bag for carrying cash, credit cards, and passports.

At night, stick to well-lit areas, especially if walking alone. While Koh Samui is known for its vibrant nightlife, it's always wise to travel with a friend or take a reputable taxi service after dark. Be cautious when accepting drinks from strangers or leaving your drink unattended in bars or clubs.

2. Traffic and Transportation

The roads in Koh Samui can be unpredictable, with narrow streets, sharp bends, and a mix of vehicles ranging from scooters to trucks. If you're renting a motorbike or scooter, always wear a helmet, drive cautiously, and ensure that the rental company provides valid insurance. Be mindful that traffic in Thailand drives on the left side of the road, which may take some adjustment if you're from a country that drives on the right.

Local transportation options include songthaews (shared pick-up trucks), taxis, and private vehicles. Negotiate fares with taxis in advance or ensure the meter is being used to avoid being overcharged.

3. Health and Medical Precautions

Koh Samui has modern medical facilities, including international-standard hospitals and clinics, but it's always a good idea to have travel insurance that covers medical emergencies. If you plan on engaging in water sports or outdoor activities, consider having additional insurance coverage for adventure activities.

It's also recommended to bring any necessary medications with you, as specific prescriptions may not be available locally. Pharmacies are common, but it's wise to have a small first-aid kit with essentials like insect repellent, sunscreen, and basic medications for gastrointestinal issues, headaches, or minor injuries.

Be cautious with street food hygiene. While Koh Samui has a vibrant street food scene, always choose stalls that look clean and have a steady stream of customers. Avoid drinking tap water; instead, stick to bottled water, which is readily available.

4. Respect Local Laws and Customs

Thailand has strict drug laws, and even small amounts of illegal substances can result in severe penalties, including imprisonment. It's essential to refrain from any involvement with illegal drugs or substances while on the island.

Smoking is prohibited in public places, including beaches, temples, and restaurants. Discarding cigarette butts on the beach can result in heavy fines. Also, avoid littering, as local authorities take cleanliness seriously in public areas.

5. Weather and Natural Hazards

The tropical climate of Koh Samui means sudden rain showers, especially during the rainy season. Flash floods can occur, particularly in low-lying areas, so always be aware of local weather warnings. If you're visiting during the monsoon season, exercise caution when swimming or engaging in water activities, as the seas can be rough.

Sun exposure is another concern, so always wear sunscreen and stay hydrated, particularly during the hot season when temperatures can soar. Be cautious with marine life, particularly when snorkeling or diving. While shark attacks are rare, jellyfish stings can be painful, so pay attention to any warning signs or advisories.

CHAPTER TWO

Beautiful Attractions and Must-Visit Spots

Beaches and Coastal Attractions of Koh Samui

Koh Samui is famous for its stunning beaches, each offering a unique blend of relaxation, activities, and natural beauty. Whether you're seeking vibrant nightlife, water sports, or quiet solitude, the island's coastline offers a diverse range of experiences. Among the most popular beaches are Chaweng Beach, Lamai Beach, and Silver Beach (Haad Thongtakian). Each of these locations has its own appeal, ensuring visitors have a variety of beach options to suit their preferences.

Chaweng Beach

Address: Chaweng, Bophut, Koh Samui, Surat Thani 84320, Thailand

Chaweng Beach is the largest and most popular beach on Koh Samui. Located on the northeastern coast of the island, it stretches for over 7 kilometers, offering white sandy shores and crystal-clear waters. It is also the most developed area on the island, with a wide variety of accommodation options, from luxury resorts to budget hostels, as well as restaurants, bars, and shops.

How to Get There:

Chaweng Beach is located about 15 minutes from Samui International Airport. You can easily reach it by taxi, motorbike, or songthaew (shared pick-up trucks used as public transport). From the airport, you can either hire a private taxi or take a songthaew, which is a more affordable option. If you're staying in nearby areas such as Bophut or Lamai, songthaews also operate between these locations.

Activities at Chaweng Beach:

1. **Swimming and Sunbathing:** The calm, shallow waters make it perfect for swimming and lounging on the beach.
2. **Water Sports:** Chaweng Beach is ideal for a variety of water sports, including jet skiing, paddleboarding, parasailing, and snorkeling. There are several rental stations along the beach.
3. **Nightlife:** Chaweng transforms into the island's nightlife hub in the evening, with a variety of beach bars, clubs, and restaurants hosting live music, fire shows, and parties.
4. **Dining:** Along the beachfront, you'll find a plethora of restaurants offering everything from local Thai cuisine to international dishes. Many restaurants offer dining right on the beach, allowing you to enjoy your meal with your toes in the sand.
5. **Shopping:** Chaweng is also known for its shopping opportunities, with street markets, boutiques, and souvenir shops offering clothes, accessories, and local handicrafts.

Lamai Beach

Address: Lamai Beach, Maret, Koh Samui, Surat Thani 84310, Thailand

Lamai Beach is the second-largest beach on Koh Samui and is located just south of Chaweng. It is a bit quieter and more relaxed compared to Chaweng Beach, offering a more laid-back atmosphere but still providing plenty of activities and entertainment. The beach itself is beautiful, with golden sand and blue waters surrounded by palm trees and rocky outcrops.

How to Get There:
Lamai Beach is about a 20-minute drive from Samui International Airport. You can reach Lamai by taxi or by renting a motorbike. Songthaews also run between Chaweng and Lamai, providing a cheap and convenient

transportation option for visitors staying in either location.

Activities at Lamai Beach:

1. **Swimming and Water Sports:** The southern part of the beach has calm, deep waters perfect for swimming, while the northern part is slightly rockier but good for snorkeling. Visitors can also enjoy jet skiing, kayaking, and paddleboarding.
2. **Massage and Spas:** There are several beachfront massage huts and spas offering traditional Thai massages, making it a great place to relax and unwind.
3. **Night Market:** Lamai has a popular night market on Sundays where you can shop for souvenirs, try local street food, and enjoy live performances.
4. **Attractions Nearby:** Close to Lamai Beach are several tourist attractions, including the iconic Grandfather and Grandmother Rocks (Hin Ta and Hin Yai), as well as the Lamai Overlap Stone, offering panoramic views of the surrounding coastline.
5. **Nightlife and Dining:** Though quieter than Chaweng, Lamai Beach has a lively nightlife scene with beachfront bars and restaurants that stay open late. There are also several beach clubs with live music, as well as traditional Thai dance performances at some of the larger resorts.

Silver Beach (Haad Thongtakian)

Address: Silver Beach, Maret, Koh Samui, Surat Thani 84310, Thailand

Silver Beach, also known as Haad Thongtakian, is a small and secluded bay located between Chaweng and Lamai beaches. This hidden gem is renowned for its tranquility, making it a perfect spot for those looking to escape the busier beaches. The beach is approximately 250 meters long and features powdery white sand and calm, clear waters surrounded by large granite boulders and lush greenery.

How to Get There:
Silver Beach is located about halfway between Chaweng and Lamai, making it easily accessible by taxi or motorbike from either location. It's about a 15-minute

drive from Chaweng and 10 minutes from Lamai. There is no public transport that directly stops at the beach, but you can hire a taxi or rent a scooter to get there. You can also ask your accommodation for a transfer or use one of the local ride-hailing apps.

Activities at Silver Beach:

1. **Snorkeling:** Silver Beach is one of the best snorkeling spots on the island, with plenty of colorful coral reefs and marine life just offshore. You can rent snorkeling gear from nearby resorts or bring your own.
2. **Swimming:** The water is calm, shallow, and perfect for swimming. The beach's sheltered location means it's protected from strong currents, making it ideal for families with children.
3. **Sunbathing and Relaxation:** With fewer crowds than Chaweng or Lamai, Silver Beach is perfect for sunbathing or simply relaxing in peace and quiet. There are a few resorts and restaurants along the beach where you can enjoy a drink or a meal while soaking in the views.
4. **Hiking and Exploring:** The surrounding area is great for exploring on foot, with several scenic hiking trails that lead up to viewpoints offering panoramic views of the coastline.

5. **Dining:** There are a handful of small, family-run restaurants and beach bars along the beach serving fresh seafood, Thai dishes, and international options. These places offer a much more intimate and relaxed dining experience compared to the larger beaches.

Each of these beaches offers something unique, catering to a variety of preferences, from vibrant, activity-packed Chaweng Beach to the quiet, serene shores of Silver Beach. Whether you're seeking an active adventure or a tranquil retreat, Koh Samui's coastal attractions have something for everyone.

Cultural and Historical Attractions of Koh Samui

Koh Samui is home to a variety of cultural and historical sites, each offering insight into the island's deep-rooted traditions and spirituality. Visitors can explore ancient temples, marvel at religious statues, and immerse themselves in the local culture. Among the most iconic sites are the Big Buddha Temple (Wat Phra Yai), Wat Plai Laem, and the intriguing Hin Ta and Hin Yai (Grandfather and Grandmother Rocks).

Big Buddha Temple (Wat Phra Yai)

Location: Northeast Koh Samui, Bo Phut, Surat Thani 84320, Thailand

The Big Buddha Temple, or Wat Phra Yai, is one of Koh Samui's most recognizable landmarks. Located on a small rocky island called Koh Phan, connected to Koh Samui by a causeway, this temple features a massive 12-meter-tall golden Buddha statue that can be seen from several kilometers away, even from the air when flying into Samui International Airport.

How to Get There:
Wat Phra Yai is located just 3 kilometers from Samui International Airport, making it a short 10-minute drive. It's also about a 15-minute drive from Chaweng Beach

and a 10-minute drive from Bophut's Fisherman's Village. You can reach the temple by taxi, rented motorbike, or songthaew. Many visitors combine their trip to Wat Phra Yai with a visit to nearby Wat Plai Laem.

What to See and Do:

1. **The Big Buddha Statue:** The main attraction is the giant seated Buddha statue, which represents enlightenment, purity, and steadfastness. Visitors can climb the stairs to the base of the statue, where they can enjoy sweeping views of the surrounding area, including Koh Phangan.
2. **Temple Complex:** Around the statue, there is a serene temple complex where visitors can explore smaller Buddha statues, offerings, and prayer halls. The area is often busy with worshippers and tourists alike, creating a vibrant atmosphere.
3. **Local Vendors and Souvenirs:** The temple grounds have several small stalls and vendors selling religious artifacts, souvenirs, clothing, and refreshments. You can purchase traditional Buddhist amulets and charms.
4. **Respectful Dress Code:** As with any temple visit in Thailand, visitors are expected to dress modestly. Shoulders and knees should be

covered, and shoes must be removed before entering temple buildings.

Wat Plai Laem

Location: Road 4171, Bo Phut, Surat Thani 84320, Thailand

Wat Plai Laem is a stunning and colorful Buddhist temple located just a few kilometers from Wat Phra Yai. Known for its intricate and vibrant designs, this temple offers a more modern depiction of Thai and Chinese religious art and architecture. The highlight of Wat Plai Laem is its 18-armed statue of Guanyin, the Goddess of

Mercy and Compassion, alongside a large white Buddha statue.

How to Get There:

Wat Plai Laem is located on the northeastern part of the island, approximately 3 kilometers from Big Buddha Temple and about 15 minutes from Chaweng Beach. It is easily accessible by taxi or motorbike. Many visitors pair a trip to Wat Plai Laem with a visit to the Big Buddha, as the two sites are close to each other.

What to See and Do:

1. **Guanyin Statue:** The 18-armed statue of Guanyin dominates the temple grounds and is a sight to behold. Guanyin is a revered figure in Chinese Buddhism, representing compassion and mercy. The design and placement of the statue make for striking photographs.
2. **The White Buddha:** In contrast to the colorful Guanyin statue, the large white Buddha statue sitting on a lotus flower adds to the spiritual aura of the temple. Visitors often light incense and make offerings at the base of the statue.
3. **Temple Grounds:** Wat Plai Laem is set amidst a picturesque lake, where visitors can feed the fish by purchasing food from the temple vendors. The peaceful surroundings offer a place of quiet reflection and serenity.

4. **Art and Architecture:** The temple buildings are beautifully adorned with murals, intricate carvings, and bright colors, showcasing a mix of traditional Thai and Chinese influences.
5. **Cultural Immersion:** While Wat Plai Laem is a popular tourist site, it remains a working temple, so visitors can observe local worshippers and participate in ceremonies if they wish.

Hin Ta and Hin Yai (Grandfather and Grandmother Rocks)

Location: South Lamai Beach, Maret, Koh Samui, Surat Thani 84310, Thailand

Hin Ta and Hin Yai, also known as the Grandfather and Grandmother Rocks, are natural rock formations located on the southern coast of Lamai Beach. These rocks have become one of Koh Samui's most visited tourist attractions due to their unusual shapes, which resemble male and female genitalia. According to local legend, the rocks represent the tragic tale of an elderly couple who, while trying to find a husband for their daughter, were shipwrecked and turned into these rocks as a symbol of their love and misfortune.

How to Get There:
The rocks are located just south of Lamai Beach, about 20 minutes from Chaweng Beach and a 30-minute drive from Koh Samui's airport. You can reach Hin Ta and Hin Yai by taxi, motorbike, or by songthaew. The entrance to the site is through a small street lined with souvenir shops and local vendors.

What to See and Do:

1. **The Rock Formations:** The primary draw is the natural rock formations, which are shaped like human genitalia. The rocks have become a popular photo spot for tourists, and their unique shapes have spawned many humorous and light-hearted stories.
2. **Scenic Views:** The area around the rocks offers beautiful views of the coastline and the sea.

There are elevated areas where visitors can take panoramic photos of the surrounding ocean and beaches.
3. **Swimming and Snorkeling:** The waters near the rocks are clear, making it a nice spot for swimming and snorkeling. Though the area can get crowded, it remains a picturesque place to spend time by the sea.
4. **Local Vendors:** The pathway leading to Hin Ta and Hin Yai is lined with vendors selling coconut-based sweets, drinks, and souvenirs. The locally famous coconut caramel candies are a must-try.
5. **Cultural Significance:** Though primarily seen as a tourist spot, the rocks are also a symbol of fertility in local culture. Visitors often leave small offerings of flowers and incense as part of local fertility rituals.

These cultural and historical attractions provide a unique glimpse into the heart of Koh Samui's traditions, beliefs, and natural wonders. From the religious significance of the Big Buddha Temple and Wat Plai Laem to the intriguing folklore surrounding the Hin Ta and Hin Yai rocks, these sites offer a rich cultural experience for tourists. Whether you're interested in religious history, art, or natural beauty, these landmarks are essential stops on any visit to Koh Samui.

Nature and Adventure in Koh Samui

Koh Samui offers a wealth of natural beauty and adventure opportunities for tourists seeking to explore its stunning landscapes and unique ecosystems. From lush waterfalls and serene gardens to vibrant marine parks, the island's natural attractions provide plenty of activities for thrill-seekers and nature lovers alike. Notable spots include Ang Thong National Marine Park, Secret Buddha Garden, Namuang Waterfalls, and Koh Taen (Coral Island).

Ang Thong National Marine Park

Location: Ang Thong National Marine Park, Gulf of Thailand, Surat Thani, Thailand

Ang Thong National Marine Park is a stunning archipelago comprising 42 islands located about 30 kilometers from Koh Samui. Known for its breathtaking limestone mountains, emerald lakes, and rich biodiversity, this marine park is a haven for nature enthusiasts and adventure seekers. The park's vibrant marine life, including colorful corals and various fish species, makes it an ideal destination for snorkeling, diving, and kayaking.

How to Get There:
Visitors typically take a day trip from Koh Samui via boat, with various tour operators offering excursions that include transportation, meals, and guided activities. The boat ride takes around 1-2 hours, depending on the chosen operator and sea conditions.

What to See and Do:

1. **Snorkeling and Diving:** The crystal-clear waters surrounding the islands are perfect for exploring underwater ecosystems teeming with marine life. Snorkeling tours often include stops at popular sites like Koh Wua Talap and Koh Mae Koh.
2. **Kayaking:** Guided kayaking tours allow visitors to paddle through the park's serene lagoons and caves, offering a unique perspective of the stunning landscapes and rock formations.

3. **Hiking:** Several hiking trails lead to stunning viewpoints, including the hike to the viewpoint on Koh Wua Talap, where visitors can enjoy panoramic views of the surrounding islands.
4. **Emerald Lake:** One of the park's highlights is the Emerald Lake (Talay Nai), a saltwater lake surrounded by steep cliffs. It's a picturesque spot for swimming and relaxing.
5. **Wildlife Spotting:** The park is home to diverse wildlife, including monkeys, sea turtles, and various bird species. Keep an eye out for these creatures while exploring the park.

Secret Buddha Garden

Location: Baan Namuang, Maret, Koh Samui, Surat Thani 84310, Thailand

The Secret Buddha Garden is a hidden gem nestled in the hills of Koh Samui. Created by a local fruit farmer, this enchanting garden is filled with over 100 statues depicting various deities, animals, and mystical creatures. Surrounded by lush vegetation and offering a tranquil atmosphere, the Secret Buddha Garden is a serene retreat away from the bustling beaches.

How to Get There:
The garden is located about 20 minutes from the main tourist areas of Chaweng and Lamai. Visitors can rent a motorbike, take a taxi, or book a guided tour. The road leading to the garden is winding and steep, making it an adventure in itself.

What to See and Do:

1. **Statue Exploration:** Wander through the garden to discover numerous statues and sculptures, each with its own unique story and significance. Many statues depict figures from Buddhist mythology, adding to the spiritual ambiance of the site.
2. **Stunning Views:** The garden is situated on a hill, offering breathtaking views of the surrounding landscape, including lush forests and distant beaches. There are several vantage points perfect for photography.
3. **Peaceful Retreat:** The serene environment makes it an ideal place for meditation or simply

enjoying the sounds of nature. Many visitors come here to escape the tourist crowds and connect with the tranquil atmosphere.
4. **Nature Walks:** Take a leisurely stroll through the garden's pathways, surrounded by tropical plants and flowers. The lush surroundings create a peaceful ambiance, perfect for relaxation.
5. **Café and Souvenirs:** There is a small café at the entrance where visitors can enjoy refreshments and purchase souvenirs to commemorate their visit.

Namuang Waterfalls

Location: Namuang Waterfall, Maret, Koh Samui, Surat Thani 84310, Thailand

Namuang Waterfalls are a pair of stunning waterfalls located in the lush interior of Koh Samui. The larger waterfall, Namuang 1, cascades over a rocky cliff into a natural pool, while Namuang 2 is smaller but equally picturesque. The falls are surrounded by dense jungle and offer a perfect spot for swimming, picnicking, and enjoying the beauty of nature.

How to Get There:
The waterfalls are located about 30 minutes from Chaweng Beach and can be accessed by car, taxi, or motorbike. The route includes a steep drive up to the falls, with parking available near the entrance.

What to See and Do:

1. **Swimming:** The pools at the base of the falls are ideal for a refreshing swim. The water is cool and inviting, making it a popular spot for both tourists and locals.
2. **Hiking:** There are several trails leading to the waterfalls, with Namuang 2 requiring a bit of hiking. The trails offer beautiful views of the surrounding jungle and opportunities to spot local wildlife.
3. **Picnicking:** Many visitors bring a picnic to enjoy amidst the natural beauty. There are shaded areas where you can relax and enjoy the sounds of the waterfalls.

4. **Adventure Activities:** For the more adventurous, there are opportunities for jungle trekking and ATV tours nearby. Some tours even include a visit to both waterfalls.
5. **Photography:** The waterfalls provide a picturesque backdrop for photos, particularly when the water flow is strong during the rainy season.

Koh Taen (Coral Island)

Location: Off the southeastern coast of Koh Samui

Koh Taen, also known as Coral Island, is a small, uninhabited island located just a short boat ride from

Koh Samui. Famous for its pristine beaches and vibrant coral reefs, Koh Taen is a popular destination for snorkeling, swimming, and relaxation in a serene setting.

How to Get There:
Visitors can reach Koh Taen via speedboat or long-tail boat, with numerous tour operators offering day trips from Koh Samui. The boat ride typically takes around 20-30 minutes.

What to See and Do:

1. **Snorkeling:** Koh Taen is renowned for its clear waters and abundant marine life. Visitors can snorkel to explore colorful coral reefs and spot various fish species, including clownfish and butterflyfish.
2. **Relaxation on the Beach:** The island features several quiet beaches where visitors can relax on soft sand, sunbathe, and enjoy the tranquility of the surroundings.
3. **Kayaking:** Some tour operators offer kayaking tours around the island, providing a unique way to explore the coastline and marine life up close.
4. **Picnic Lunches:** Many day tours include a picnic lunch on the beach, allowing guests to enjoy a meal with a view of the ocean.
5. **Wildlife Spotting:** The island is home to various bird species, and visitors may also spot monitor

lizards and other wildlife while exploring the beaches and coastal areas.

Koh Samui's natural attractions provide ample opportunities for adventure and exploration, from stunning national parks to serene waterfalls and pristine islands. Whether you seek thrilling outdoor activities, breathtaking scenery, or simply a peaceful retreat in nature, Koh Samui offers a diverse range of experiences that will enhance any traveler's journey. Each of these destinations showcases the island's natural beauty, inviting visitors to connect with the lush landscapes and rich ecosystems that make Koh Samui a true tropical paradise.

CHAPTER THREE

Hidden Gems and Off-the-Beaten-Path Attractions

Lesser-Known Beaches in Koh Samui

While Koh Samui is famous for its bustling tourist beaches like Chaweng and Lamai, the island also boasts several lesser-known beaches that offer tranquility, stunning views, and a more laid-back atmosphere. Two of these hidden gems are Taling Ngam Beach and Lipa Noi Beach. Both beaches provide a perfect escape for those looking to relax away from the crowds.

Taling Ngam Beach

Location: Taling Ngam, Koh Samui, Surat Thani, Thailand

Taling Ngam Beach is a serene stretch of coastline located on the southwestern side of Koh Samui. This beach is known for its picturesque sunsets, soft white sand, and stunning views of the nearby islands, including Koh Madsum and Koh Tan. The beach is less developed than other areas, making it ideal for visitors seeking a peaceful retreat.

How to Get There:

Taling Ngam Beach is about a 30-minute drive from the popular Chaweng area. Visitors can rent a car, motorbike, or take a taxi. The road leading to the beach is scenic, with views of the lush hills and coconut plantations.

What to See and Do:

1. **Relaxation:** The beach offers a tranquil setting perfect for sunbathing, reading, or simply enjoying the gentle sounds of the waves. The soft sand and clear waters provide a relaxing atmosphere away from the busy tourist spots.
2. **Sunset Viewing:** Taling Ngam is renowned for its breathtaking sunsets. Many visitors come here in the evening to watch the sky transform into a

palette of vibrant colors as the sun dips below the horizon.
3. **Dining:** While there are fewer dining options directly on the beach, some beach clubs and restaurants offer delicious local cuisine with beautiful views. Guests can enjoy fresh seafood and traditional Thai dishes.
4. **Water Activities:** Though less commercialized, there are opportunities for kayaking and paddleboarding in the calm waters, providing a chance to explore the coastline and enjoy the scenic surroundings.
5. **Local Culture:** The area surrounding Taling Ngam is less touristy, allowing visitors to experience the local way of life. Strolling through the nearby fishing villages offers insight into the island's culture and traditions.

Lipa Noi Beach

Location: Lipa Noi, Koh Samui, Surat Thani, Thailand

Lipa Noi Beach is a stunning, family-friendly beach located on the west coast of Koh Samui. Known for its long stretch of soft, white sand and shallow waters, it's an ideal spot for families with children. The beach is less crowded than the more popular beaches, making it perfect for relaxation and fun in the sun.

How to Get There:
Lipa Noi Beach is approximately a 30-minute drive from Chaweng Beach. Visitors can reach it by renting a car, motorbike, or taking a taxi. The route is scenic and straightforward, providing lovely views of the island along the way.

What to See and Do:

1. **Swimming:** The shallow waters make Lipa Noi Beach perfect for swimming, especially for families with young children. The calm sea allows for safe and enjoyable playtime in the water.
2. **Sunbathing and Relaxation:** The soft sands are ideal for sunbathing and relaxing with a good book. Visitors can spread out on beach towels or rent sun loungers for a comfortable day by the sea.
3. **Dining:** There are several beachfront restaurants and bars where guests can enjoy meals and drinks with ocean views. Fresh seafood and Thai dishes are popular choices.
4. **Water Sports:** Lipa Noi offers opportunities for various water sports, including paddleboarding and kayaking. Rentals are available at local shops, allowing visitors to explore the coastline.
5. **Beachfront Accommodation:** Lipa Noi features several hotels and resorts right on the beach, providing a perfect location for visitors looking to unwind and enjoy the beautiful scenery.

Taling Ngam Beach and Lipa Noi Beach showcase the quieter side of Koh Samui, inviting travelers to escape the hustle and bustle of the more touristy areas. These beaches offer stunning natural beauty, serene environments, and opportunities for relaxation and family fun, making them perfect destinations for those looking to experience a more peaceful side of the island. Whether you're watching the sunset at Taling Ngam or enjoying a family day at Lipa Noi, these lesser-known beaches promise memorable moments in paradise.

Secret Spots for Nature Lovers in Koh Samui

Koh Samui is not only famous for its pristine beaches and vibrant nightlife but also for its lush landscapes and hidden natural gems. For nature lovers seeking tranquility away from the tourist crowds, the Overlap Stone and the Magic Garden (Tarnim Magic Garden) are two must-visit spots that offer unique experiences amidst the island's stunning natural beauty.

Overlap Stone

Location: Near Baan Taling Ngam, Koh Samui, Surat Thani, Thailand

Overlap Stone is a fascinating natural formation located on the southern coast of Koh Samui. This unique rock formation stands out due to its peculiar appearance, where large stones seem to balance on top of one another, creating an impressive sight. The area surrounding the Overlap Stone is also rich in lush greenery, offering a peaceful atmosphere that invites exploration and contemplation.

How to Get There:
To reach Overlap Stone, visitors can take a short drive from Taling Ngam Beach. The best way is to rent a car or scooter. The drive to the location is scenic, with views of the coastline and hills. Once there, a short trek through the tropical forest leads to the stone formation.

What to See and Do:

1. **Photography:** The Overlap Stone provides a perfect backdrop for photography enthusiasts. The contrast between the rugged stones and the vibrant greenery makes for stunning images.
2. **Nature Walks:** The surrounding area is rich in biodiversity, with various tropical plants and wildlife. Exploring the trails near Overlap Stone offers an opportunity to enjoy nature and discover the local flora and fauna.
3. **Picnicking:** The serene environment makes it a great spot for a peaceful picnic. Visitors can pack a meal and enjoy it amidst nature, surrounded by the soothing sounds of birds and rustling leaves.
4. **Quiet Reflection:** The tranquility of the location makes it an ideal spot for quiet reflection or meditation. The natural beauty and calm atmosphere can provide a much-needed escape from the hustle of everyday life.

Magic Garden (Tarnim Magic Garden)

Location: Near Ban Tai, Koh Samui, Surat Thani, Thailand

Tarnim Magic Garden, commonly known as the Magic Garden, is an enchanting hidden gem nestled in the hills of Koh Samui. This whimsical garden is home to a collection of colorful statues, stone sculptures, and lush gardens, all designed and created by a local artist. The garden is a testament to creativity and imagination, making it a delightful destination for visitors of all ages.

How to Get There:
Magic Garden is located about a 30-minute drive from Chaweng Beach. Visitors can reach it by renting a car or scooter or by hiring a taxi. The drive through the scenic

hills adds to the allure of the visit. A short walk through the garden's pathways leads to the various sculptures and art installations.

What to See and Do:

1. **Exploring the Sculptures:** The garden features a variety of colorful and unique sculptures, including whimsical characters and mythical creatures. Each piece tells a story, making the garden a fascinating place to explore.
2. **Photography:** The vibrant colors and artistic designs create perfect opportunities for photography. Visitors can capture the beauty of the sculptures against the backdrop of lush greenery.
3. **Nature Walks:** In addition to the art, the surrounding landscape is filled with tropical plants and trees, inviting visitors to enjoy leisurely walks while soaking in the natural beauty of Koh Samui.
4. **Picnic Areas:** There are several spots within the garden where visitors can relax and enjoy a picnic surrounded by the enchanting scenery. It's a great place to unwind and enjoy the peaceful atmosphere.
5. **Cultural Insight:** The Magic Garden reflects the creative spirit of Koh Samui and offers visitors a glimpse into the local culture and artistry.

Engaging with the art can provide deeper insight into the island's artistic community.

For nature lovers exploring Koh Samui, the Overlap Stone and the Magic Garden present unique and tranquil experiences that showcase the island's diverse beauty. Whether you are marveling at the natural formations of Overlap Stone or wandering through the whimsical landscapes of the Magic Garden, these secret spots provide a perfect escape into nature, allowing visitors to connect with the island's serene environment and artistic heritage.

Adventure Opportunities in Koh Samui

Koh Samui is not just a paradise for beach lovers; it also offers a myriad of adventure opportunities for thrill-seekers and outdoor enthusiasts. From traversing the island's lush jungles to soaring through the treetops, the adventure experiences available on this stunning island are sure to provide unforgettable memories. Two popular activities that capture the adventurous spirit of Koh Samui are Off-Road Jungle Safari and Zip-lining and Canopy Adventures.

Off-Road Jungle Safari

Overview:

The Off-Road Jungle Safari is an exhilarating way to explore the rugged terrain and breathtaking landscapes of Koh Samui. This adventure takes participants deep into the island's jungle, where they can witness its rich biodiversity, stunning waterfalls, and panoramic views from hilltops.

How It Works:

Participants typically ride in 4x4 vehicles or ATVs, guided by experienced instructors who know the best trails and hidden spots. Tours can vary in duration, often lasting from half a day to a full day, and usually include visits to key attractions.

What to See and Do:

1. **Waterfalls:** Most jungle safari tours include stops at famous waterfalls, such as Namuang Waterfall, where visitors can take a refreshing dip in natural pools or enjoy a picnic amidst the serene surroundings.
2. **Stunning Viewpoints:** Adventurers can experience breathtaking views from high vantage points, offering photo opportunities of the lush jungle, coastal scenery, and nearby islands.

3. **Local Wildlife:** The jungle is home to diverse flora and fauna, providing opportunities to spot unique wildlife, including tropical birds, monkeys, and various species of plants.
4. **Cultural Experiences:** Some tours incorporate visits to local villages, allowing participants to learn about traditional Thai culture and the daily lives of the residents.

Tips for Participants:

- Wear comfortable clothing and sturdy shoes, as the terrain can be uneven and muddy.
- Bring sunscreen, insect repellent, and a hat for protection against the sun.
- A camera or smartphone is recommended to capture the stunning scenery.

Zip-lining and Canopy Adventures

Zip-lining and canopy adventures offer an adrenaline-pumping experience that allows visitors to glide through the treetops of Koh Samui's lush jungles. This thrilling activity provides a unique perspective of the island's beautiful landscape, combining adventure with the chance to connect with nature.

How It Works:
Zip-lining tours usually include a series of ziplines strung between platforms in the trees, allowing participants to soar above the ground while enjoying breathtaking views. Most tours are led by professional guides who ensure safety and provide instruction.

What to See and Do:

1. **Canopy Views:** Zip-lining gives participants a bird's-eye view of the jungle canopy, showcasing the vibrant greenery and wildlife below. Some courses offer stunning vistas of the surrounding hills and coastline.
2. **Suspension Bridges:** Many zip-lining tours include walking across suspension bridges that connect the treetops, adding to the excitement of the experience. These bridges offer a thrilling

way to experience the height while surrounded by nature.
3. **Adventure Challenges:** Some zip-lining courses incorporate additional adventure activities, such as rope courses or climbing elements, for those looking for a more comprehensive experience.
4. **Wildlife Spotting:** While zip-lining, participants may spot local wildlife, such as monkeys, birds, and other creatures that inhabit the jungles of Koh Samui.

Tips for Participants:

- Dress comfortably, avoiding loose clothing that could get caught during the zip-lining.
- Closed-toed shoes are essential for safety.
- Listen carefully to the guides for safety instructions and tips on how to maximize the experience.

Koh Samui is a playground for adventure enthusiasts, offering thrilling activities like Off-Road Jungle Safaris and Zip-lining and Canopy Adventures. Whether navigating the island's rugged trails or soaring through the treetops, these experiences allow visitors to explore Koh Samui's stunning natural beauty while satisfying their thirst for adventure. Embrace the spirit of exploration and create unforgettable memories in this tropical paradise.

CHAPTER FOUR

Food and Cuisine

Must-Try Local Dishes in Koh Samui

Koh Samui's culinary scene is a vibrant blend of traditional Thai flavors and local ingredients, making it a paradise for food lovers. Here are some must-try local dishes that showcase the unique tastes of the island, along with recommendations on where to enjoy them.

Tom Yam Goong

Description:
Tom Yam Goong is a famous Thai soup known for its bold flavors and aromatic ingredients. This spicy and sour soup features succulent shrimp (goong), fresh herbs like lemongrass, galangal, and kaffir lime leaves, along with mushrooms and chili peppers. The combination of sweet, sour, salty, and spicy flavors creates a delightful balance that is both refreshing and satisfying.

Where to Try:

- **Jungle Club Koh Samui**
  Located on a hill with breathtaking views of the

island, Jungle Club offers a fantastic Tom Yam Goong made with fresh ingredients. The beautiful setting complements the delicious food, making it a perfect dining experience.
- **Samui Seafood Grill**
  This beachfront restaurant in Chaweng serves an authentic version of Tom Yam Goong, using fresh shrimp and local herbs. Enjoy the lively atmosphere and beautiful sea views while savoring this iconic dish.

Som Tum (Green Papaya Salad)

Description:
Som Tum is a refreshing Thai salad made from shredded green papaya, tomatoes, green beans, and peanuts, all tossed in a spicy and tangy dressing of lime juice, fish sauce, and palm sugar. It is often served with a side of sticky rice and grilled chicken or fish. This dish is celebrated for its vibrant flavors and is a staple of Thai cuisine.

Where to Try:

- **Krua Baan Thai**
  Located in Lamai, Krua Baan Thai is known for its authentic Som Tum. The salad is made fresh

to order, allowing you to adjust the spice level to your liking.
- **Lamai Night Market**
  The night market in Lamai offers several stalls where you can find delicious Som Tum. The vendors prepare it right in front of you, allowing you to enjoy the lively atmosphere while indulging in this local favorite.

Pad Thai

Description:

Pad Thai is a beloved stir-fried noodle dish that combines rice noodles with tofu, shrimp, or chicken, along with eggs, bean sprouts, and peanuts, all tossed in a flavorful sauce made from tamarind paste, fish sauce, and sugar. This dish is often garnished with lime wedges and fresh herbs, making it a perfect balance of sweet, salty, and tangy flavors.

Where to Try:

- **Pad Thai Thip Samai**
  This iconic eatery in Chaweng is famous for its delicious Pad Thai. The chefs prepare it using traditional methods, ensuring each plate is packed with flavor. Don't forget to try their signature version with prawns!

- **The Cliff Bar and Grill**
  Perched on a hillside, this restaurant offers stunning sunset views along with a delectable Pad Thai. The ambiance is perfect for a romantic dinner or a night out with friends.

Thai Coconut Soup (Tom Kha Gai)

Description:
Tom Kha Gai is a rich and creamy coconut soup featuring tender chicken, mushrooms, and fragrant herbs like galangal and lemongrass. The combination of coconut milk, lime juice, and chili creates a comforting and aromatic dish that is both savory and slightly sweet. It's perfect for those who love the soothing flavors of coconut.

Where to Try:

- **Coco Tam's**
  This beachside restaurant in Bophut is renowned for its delicious Tom Kha Gai. With a vibrant atmosphere and stunning beach views, it's a great place to enjoy this comforting soup while soaking in the beauty of Koh Samui.
- **The Spice Route**
  Located in Chaweng, The Spice Route serves a delicious version of Tom Kha Gai, prepared with fresh ingredients. The restaurant's cozy

atmosphere makes it an excellent spot to enjoy this warm and flavorful dish.

Best Restaurants in Koh Samui

Koh Samui boasts a diverse culinary scene that caters to all tastes, from fine dining establishments serving gourmet dishes to vibrant street food markets offering authentic local flavors. Here's a guide to some of the best dining options on the island, along with details on how to find them.

Fine Dining Options

1. *Dining on the Rocks*

Overview: Located at the Six Senses Samui Resort, Dining on the Rocks offers a breathtaking dining experience with panoramic views of the Gulf of Thailand. This award-winning restaurant is known for its innovative menu featuring a fusion of Thai and international cuisine, all prepared with fresh, local ingredients.

Address: Six Senses Samui, 9/10 Moo 5, Baan Tai, Koh Samui, Surat Thani 84140, Thailand

How to Get There: From Chaweng, take the main road towards Bophut and then head towards the north coast of the island. It's about a 30-minute drive. Reservations are recommended for this upscale dining experience.

2. *The Cliff Bar and Grill*

Overview: Perched on a cliff overlooking the ocean, The Cliff Bar and Grill is renowned for its stunning sunset views and gourmet dishes. The menu offers a mix of Thai and Western cuisine, with an emphasis on fresh seafood. The ambiance is both romantic and elegant, making it a perfect spot for a special occasion.

Address: The Cliff Bar and Grill, 9/99 Moo 1, Bophut, Koh Samui, Surat Thani 84320, Thailand

How to Get There: Located in Bophut, The Cliff is easily accessible by car or taxi from Chaweng, approximately a 15-minute drive. The restaurant is situated on the main road along the coast, making it easy to find.

3. *Zazen Restaurant*

Overview: Zazen Restaurant offers a unique fine dining experience set in a tranquil garden setting by the beach. The menu features a delightful mix of Thai and international cuisine, with an emphasis on fresh ingredients and beautifully presented dishes. The romantic atmosphere is enhanced by candlelight and gentle ocean breezes.

Address: Zazen Boutique Resort & Spa, 177 Moo 1, Bophut, Koh Samui, Surat Thani 84320, Thailand

How to Get There: From Chaweng, head north along the coast for about 15 minutes. Zazen is located in Bophut, close to Fisherman's Village. Reservations are advisable for dinner, especially during peak season.

Local Street Food and Market Experiences

1. *Lamai Night Market*
Overview: The Lamai Night Market is a bustling hub of street food, offering a variety of local delicacies, including fresh seafood, grilled meats, and delicious Thai desserts. It's a great place to experience authentic Thai flavors in a lively atmosphere. The market comes alive in the evenings, making it a popular spot for both locals and tourists.

Address: Lamai Beach, Koh Samui, Surat Thani 84310, Thailand

How to Get There: Located along the main road in Lamai, the night market is easily accessible by foot if you're staying in the area. Alternatively, you can take a taxi from Chaweng, which is about a 20-minute drive. The market typically opens around 5 PM and runs until late evening.

2. *Fisherman's Village Walking Street*

Overview: Held every Friday evening, Fisherman's Village Walking Street in Bophut transforms into a vibrant street market filled with food stalls, shops, and live entertainment. Here, you can find a wide range of street food, including Thai curries, spring rolls, and fresh fruit shakes. The lively atmosphere and beautiful beach setting make this market a must-visit.

Address: Fisherman's Village, Bophut, Koh Samui, Surat Thani 84320, Thailand

How to Get There: Fisherman's Village is located in Bophut, about a 15-minute drive from Chaweng. If you're in the area, simply walk to the village on Fridays when the market is open. Parking can be found nearby but may be limited, so consider arriving early.

3. *Chaweng Night Market*

Overview: Chaweng Night Market is another bustling spot for street food enthusiasts, offering a plethora of options ranging from traditional Thai dishes to international fare. You'll find everything from barbecued seafood to delectable desserts. The market has a lively atmosphere, making it a great place to mingle with locals and other travelers.

Address: Chaweng Beach, Koh Samui, Surat Thani 84320, Thailand

How to Get There: Chaweng Night Market is conveniently located along the main road in Chaweng, making it easily accessible by foot or taxi. The market typically opens in the late afternoon and runs until late at night, with the busiest hours being from 7 PM onward.

Koh Samui's dining scene is diverse, offering everything from high-end culinary experiences to vibrant street food markets. Whether you prefer the elegance of fine dining or the casual atmosphere of local markets, you will find a variety of delicious options to satisfy your palate. Enjoy exploring the rich flavors of Koh Samui as you embark on your culinary journey!

Vegetarian and Vegan Food Options in Koh Samui

Koh Samui is increasingly accommodating to vegetarian and vegan diets, with numerous restaurants and cafés offering delicious plant-based options. Here are some notable places to enjoy healthy and flavorful vegetarian and vegan meals:

1. *The Sanctuary Thailand*

Overview: Nestled on the serene shores of Koh Phangan, The Sanctuary Thailand is not just a wellness resort but also a renowned restaurant offering a fully vegan and vegetarian menu. The dishes are made from fresh, organic ingredients, emphasizing health and flavor. Signature offerings include vegan Buddha bowls, smoothies, and a variety of gluten-free options.

Address: The Sanctuary Thailand, 18/1 Moo 6, Baantai, Koh Phangan, Surat Thani 84280, Thailand

How to Get There: While technically on Koh Phangan, The Sanctuary is just a short boat ride from Koh Samui. From Samui, take a ferry from Bangrak Pier to Koh Phangan, and then a taxi to the resort.

2. *Luna Lounge*

Overview: Located in Bang Po, Luna Lounge offers a wide range of vegetarian and vegan options, including salads, wraps, and pizzas. The relaxed atmosphere and sea views make it a great spot for lunch or dinner. They also feature a variety of plant-based smoothies and desserts.

Address: Luna Lounge, 93/3 Moo 4, Bang Po, Koh Samui, Surat Thani 84140, Thailand

How to Get There: From Chaweng, take the main road north towards Bang Po. The restaurant is approximately a 30-minute drive. Look for signage along the beachfront road.

3. *The Living Room* at The Samui Mermaid

Overview: The Living Room is a popular restaurant at The Samui Mermaid that offers a range of vegetarian and vegan options, including salads, pastas, and Thai-inspired dishes. They pride themselves on using fresh, local ingredients to create vibrant, healthy meals.

Address: The Samui Mermaid, 78/1 Moo 3, Chaweng Beach, Koh Samui, Surat Thani 84320, Thailand

How to Get There: Located in Chaweng, The Living Room is easily accessible by foot or taxi from most hotels in the area. It's just a short drive from Chaweng Beach, making it a convenient stop for delicious vegetarian meals.

4. *Samui Institute of Thai Culinary Arts (SITCA)*

Overview: While primarily a cooking school, SITCA also offers a café where visitors can enjoy vegetarian and vegan meals. The menu changes regularly and includes various plant-based dishes that reflect traditional Thai cuisine, showcasing the versatility of vegetarian cooking.

Address: Samui Institute of Thai Culinary Arts, 48/14 Moo 4, Bophut, Koh Samui, Surat Thani 84320, Thailand

How to Get There: From Chaweng, head north along the coast to Bophut. SITCA is located on the main road, making it easily accessible by car or taxi, approximately a 15-minute drive.

Popular Cafés and Coffee Spots in Koh Samui

Koh Samui is home to many charming cafés that offer a cozy atmosphere for enjoying coffee, tea, and light bites. Here are some popular spots worth checking out:

1. *Café 69*

Overview: Café 69 is a trendy spot in Chaweng that serves a mix of Thai and Western dishes, along with excellent coffee and fresh juices. The vibrant decor and relaxed atmosphere make it a great place for breakfast or a casual lunch.

Address: Café 69, 69/3 Moo 2, Chaweng Beach, Koh Samui, Surat Thani 84320, Thailand

How to Get There: Café 69 is centrally located in Chaweng, easily accessible by foot or taxi. It's a great stop after a morning on the beach.

2. *The Coffee Club*

Overview: Part of a well-known chain, The Coffee Club offers a wide range of coffee drinks, smoothies, and light meals. The relaxed ambiance and free Wi-Fi make it an ideal spot for working or unwinding with a good book.

Address: The Coffee Club, Chaweng, Koh Samui, Surat Thani 84320, Thailand

How to Get There: Located on Chaweng Beach Road, it's a convenient stop for anyone in the area. Look for it near the main shopping area of Chaweng.

3. *The Jungle Café*

Overview:The Jungle Café is a hidden gem located in the heart of Lamai. Surrounded by lush greenery, this café offers a peaceful escape where visitors can enjoy fresh coffee, smoothies, and a variety of health-conscious food options.

Address: The Jungle Café, 146/1 Moo 3, Lamai, Koh Samui, Surat Thani 84310, Thailand

How to Get There: From Lamai Beach, it's a short walk or a quick taxi ride. The café is tucked away off the main road, providing a tranquil setting for a refreshing break.

4. *Baan Haad Rin* Café*

Overview: Located near Haad Rin Beach, Baan Haad Rin offers a casual atmosphere with great coffee and light meals. It's a perfect spot to relax after a day at the beach or before heading out to explore.

Address: Baan Haad Rin, 56/1 Moo 6, Haad Rin, Koh Phangan, Surat Thani 84280, Thailand

How to Get There: Although located on Koh Phangan, Baan Haad Rin is accessible by ferry from Koh Samui. After arriving at Haad Rin, it's just a short walk to the café.

Koh Samui offers a delightful range of vegetarian and vegan options alongside popular cafés perfect for enjoying a relaxing meal or a cup of coffee. Whether you're looking for healthy plant-based cuisine or a cozy spot to unwind, the island has something to satisfy every palate. Enjoy your culinary exploration in this beautiful tropical paradise!

CHAPTER FIVE

Accommodation Options on Koh Samui

Recommended Hotels for Every Budget in Koh Samui

Koh Samui offers a wide range of accommodations to suit every traveler's needs and budget. Below are recommendations for luxury resorts, mid-range hotels, and budget-friendly options, complete with addresses and directions on how to get there.

Luxury Resorts

1. Four Seasons Resort Koh Samui

Overview: This stunning resort is set on a private beach and surrounded by lush gardens. Guests can enjoy luxurious villas, a world-class spa, and exquisite dining options.

Address: Four Seasons Resort Koh Samui, 219 Moo 5, Ang Thong, Koh Samui, Surat Thani 84140, Thailand

How to Get There: From Samui International Airport, it's approximately a 30-minute drive. Taxis and private transfers are readily available at the airport.

2. Banyan Tree Samui

Nestled in a secluded cove, this resort features luxurious pool villas with breathtaking ocean views. Guests can indulge in a spa, fitness center, and gourmet dining.

Address: Banyan Tree Samui, 99/4 Moo 4, Maret, Koh Samui, Surat Thani 84310, Thailand

How to Get There: A 30-minute taxi ride from Samui International Airport will take you directly to the resort.

3. Conrad Koh Samui

Overview: This upscale resort boasts contemporary villas with private pools, offering stunning sunset views. Guests can enjoy fine dining, a lavish spa, and various recreational activities.

Address: Conrad Koh Samui, 49/8-9 Moo 4, A. Koh Samui, Surat Thani 84140, Thailand

How to Get There: From Samui International Airport, it's about a 45-minute drive to the resort, which can be arranged through hotel transfers or taxis.

4. The Ritz-Carlton, Koh Samui

Overview: Offering elegant accommodations and exceptional service, this resort features private villas, an extensive spa, and gourmet dining.

Address: The Ritz-Carlton, Koh Samui, 174/3 Moo 4, Taling Ngam, Koh Samui, Surat Thani 84140, Thailand

How to Get There: A 45-minute drive from the airport will take you to the resort, with taxis available at the airport.

Mid-Range Hotels

1. Amari Koh Samui

Overview: This beachfront hotel offers comfortable rooms and suites with modern amenities. The on-site dining options and spa services make it a great choice for relaxation.

Address: Amari Koh Samui, 14/3 Moo 2, Chaweng Beach, Koh Samui, Surat Thani 84320, Thailand

How to Get There: From Samui International Airport, it's a quick 10-minute taxi ride to the hotel.

2. Chaweng Regent Beach Resort

Overview: Set on Chaweng Beach, this resort features well-appointed rooms, multiple pools, and dining options. Its prime location offers easy access to nightlife and shopping.

Address: Chaweng Regent Beach Resort, 155/4 Chaweng Beach, Koh Samui, Surat Thani 84320, Thailand

How to Get There: A 15-minute drive from the airport will take you to the resort, accessible via taxi or hotel transfer.

3. The Sarann

Overview: This boutique hotel offers stylish accommodations and a peaceful atmosphere. The infinity pool and on-site restaurant provide a relaxing retreat.

Address: The Sarann, 111/1 Moo 6, Chaweng Noi Beach, Koh Samui, Surat Thani 84310, Thailand

How to Get There: From the airport, it's about a 20-minute taxi ride to the hotel.

4. Samui Paradise Chaweng Beach Resort

Overview: This charming resort features a beautiful beachfront location with comfortable rooms and a variety of amenities, including a restaurant and swimming pool.

Address: Samui Paradise Chaweng Beach Resort, 14/2 Moo 2, Chaweng Beach, Koh Samui, Surat Thani 84320, Thailand

How to Get There: A 10-minute drive from Samui International Airport will take you to the resort.

Budget-Friendly Options

1. Green Hotel

Overview: A budget-friendly hotel offering comfortable accommodations and a friendly atmosphere. Guests can enjoy simple rooms and easy access to the beach.

Address: Green Hotel, 60/8 Moo 2, Chaweng Beach, Koh Samui, Surat Thani 84320, Thailand

How to Get There: From the airport, it's a quick 10-minute taxi ride to the hotel.

2. Chaweng Beach Hotel

Overview: Located near the vibrant Chaweng Beach, this hotel offers affordable rooms and easy access to local attractions, making it an ideal spot for budget travelers.

Address: Chaweng Beach Hotel, 99/99 Moo 2, Chaweng Beach, Koh Samui, Surat Thani 84320, Thailand

How to Get There: A 10-minute drive from Samui International Airport will take you to the hotel.

3. Lamai Buri Resort

Overview: This resort offers budget accommodations with a laid-back atmosphere, featuring a swimming pool and proximity to Lamai Beach.

Address: Lamai Buri Resort, 153/4 Moo 4, Lamai Beach, Koh Samui, Surat Thani 84310, Thailand

How to Get There: From the airport, it's about a 30-minute taxi ride to the resort.

4. Baan Haad Rin Resort

Overview: This resort provides affordable beachfront accommodations, perfect for those looking to explore the famous Haad Rin Beach and its vibrant nightlife.

Address: Baan Haad Rin Resort, 56/2 Moo 6, Haad Rin Beach, Koh Phangan, Surat Thani 84280, Thailand

How to Get There: Take a ferry from Koh Samui to Koh Phangan, and the resort is a short taxi ride from the ferry terminal.

Koh Samui caters to every budget, offering a range of accommodations from luxury resorts to budget-friendly options. Whether you're seeking a lavish getaway or a comfortable stay without breaking the bank, you'll find the perfect hotel to suit your needs on this beautiful island.

Unique Stays and Boutique Accommodations in Koh Samui

For travelers seeking a distinctive experience, Koh Samui offers a variety of unique stays and boutique accommodations that go beyond the traditional hotel experience. From beachfront villas to private rentals, these options provide a personal touch and the chance to immerse oneself in the island's beauty.

1. The Librarian Koh Samui

Overview: The Librarian is a chic boutique hotel located on Chaweng Noi Beach, offering a tranquil atmosphere and a unique design that blends modern luxury with traditional Thai elements. Guests can enjoy an extensive library, personalized service, and easy access to the beach.

Address: The Librarian Koh Samui, 35/2 Chaweng Noi Beach, Koh Samui, Surat Thani 84310, Thailand

How to Get There: A 15-minute taxi ride from Samui International Airport will bring you to this boutique hotel.

Unique Features: The hotel features a stunning infinity pool overlooking the ocean, beautifully designed rooms with private balconies, and a focus on wellness with yoga and spa services.

---

2. Baan Haad Rin Resort

Overview: Located near the famous Full Moon Party area, Baan Haad Rin Resort offers a mix of vibrant atmosphere and beachfront relaxation. This resort features traditional Thai-style bungalows, providing a cozy and authentic experience.

Address: Baan Haad Rin Resort, 56/2 Moo 6, Haad Rin Beach, Koh Phangan, Surat Thani 84280, Thailand

How to Get There: Take a ferry from Koh Samui to Koh Phangan, followed by a short taxi ride to the resort.

Unique Features: Guests can enjoy a beachfront location with easy access to nightlife and local attractions, along with personalized service and a friendly atmosphere.

---

3. The Sunset Beach Resort & Spa

Overview: This boutique resort features stylish villas and suites, each with stunning ocean views. The Sunset Beach Resort is known for its serene ambiance and focus on sustainability, making it a great choice for eco-conscious travelers.

Address: The Sunset Beach Resort & Spa, 101/1 Moo 4, Maret, Koh Samui, Surat Thani 84310, Thailand

How to Get There: Approximately 30 minutes by taxi from Samui International Airport.

Unique Features*:* The resort boasts an organic restaurant, a full-service spa, and numerous wellness programs, including yoga and meditation sessions.

---

4. Samui Mountain Village

Overview: Perched on the hillsides of Koh Samui, Samui Mountain Village offers breathtaking views and unique accommodation options ranging from luxurious villas to cozy bungalows. This property provides a tranquil escape from the busy beaches while remaining close to local attractions.

Address: Samui Mountain Village, 88/8 Moo 5, Taling Ngam, Koh Samui, Surat Thani 84140, Thailand

How to Get There: About a 40-minute drive from Samui International Airport, this location can be reached via taxi or hotel transfer.

Unique Features: Guests can enjoy private pools, lush gardens, and a peaceful environment, along with opportunities for hiking and exploring the surrounding nature.

5. Private Beachfront Villas

Overview: Koh Samui is home to several private beachfront villas available for rent, offering guests the ultimate in luxury and privacy. These villas come fully equipped with modern amenities, private pools, and stunning ocean views, providing a home away from home.

Examples of Villas:

- **Villa M**
  Address: 101/15 Moo 4, Taling Ngam, Koh Samui, Surat Thani 84140, Thailand
  How to Get There: Approximately a 40-minute drive from Samui International Airport.
  Features: Modern design, large outdoor spaces, and direct beach access.
- **The View Villa**
  Address: 104/24 Moo 5, Bophut, Koh Samui, Surat Thani 84320, Thailand
  How to Get There: About a 15-minute drive from Samui International Airport.
  Features: Panoramic views, infinity pool, and proximity to Fisherman's Village.

6. Eco-Friendly Boutique Hotels

The Art Resort

Overview: Set within an artistic atmosphere, The Art Resort offers beautifully decorated rooms with a focus on eco-friendly practices. This boutique hotel is perfect for art lovers and those seeking a sustainable stay.

Address: The Art Resort, 7/9 Moo 1, Bang Por, Koh Samui, Surat Thani 84330, Thailand

How to Get There: A 30-minute taxi ride from Samui International Airport.

Unique Features: The hotel showcases local artwork, has a small gallery on-site, and promotes sustainable tourism through various eco-friendly initiatives.

Koh Samui's unique stays and boutique accommodations offer a range of experiences for travelers looking to immerse themselves in the island's charm and beauty. Whether you prefer a luxurious villa, an eco-friendly hotel, or a cozy bungalow, Koh Samui provides options that cater to diverse tastes and budgets, ensuring a memorable stay.

CHAPTER SIX

Transportation and Travel Logistics

Getting to Koh Samui

Traveling to Koh Samui is relatively straightforward, thanks to its well-connected transport links. Whether you're coming from mainland Thailand or another international destination, there are several convenient options to reach this beautiful island.

Airlines Serving Koh Samui

Koh Samui is serviced by several airlines that provide direct flights from various locations, making it accessible for both international and domestic travelers. The main airport on the island is Samui International Airport (USM), which is known for its unique open-air design and tropical gardens.

1. Bangkok Airways

- **Overview:** As the main carrier to Koh Samui, Bangkok Airways operates numerous flights daily from Bangkok (Suvarnabhumi Airport) and other major Thai cities.
- **Destinations:**

- **Bangkok (BKK):** Approximately 1 hour and 15 minutes flight time.
- **Chiang Mai (CNX):** Offers seasonal flights to Koh Samui.
- **Phuket (HKT):** Provides a direct connection to the island.

2. Thai Airways

- **Overview:** Thai Airways operates flights to Koh Samui from Bangkok as part of a codeshare agreement with Bangkok Airways.
- **Destinations:**
- **Bangkok (BKK):** Regular flights available.

3. AirAsia

- **Overview:** AirAsia provides flights from Bangkok and other regional cities, though they typically land in Surat Thani or Nakhon Si Thammarat. Passengers must then take a bus to the ferry terminal for transport to Koh Samui.
- **Destinations:**
- **Bangkok (DMK):** Multiple flights daily.

4. International Airlines

- **Overview:** Several international airlines offer flights to Samui via Bangkok. These may include

connecting flights from various cities worldwide, including London, Sydney, and Kuala Lumpur. Some of the airlines are:
- **Qatar Airways, Singapore Airlines, and Emirates** have connections to Bangkok from international destinations, allowing seamless travel to Koh Samui.

5. Other Domestic Airlines

- **Nok Air and Lion Air:** These budget airlines operate routes from regional cities to Surat Thani, followed by bus and ferry transfers to Koh Samui.

Ferry Services

For travelers already in mainland Thailand, ferries are a popular option for reaching Koh Samui. There are two main ferry operators providing services to the island, ensuring convenient and frequent transfers.

1. Seatran Ferry

- **Overview:** Seatran Ferry offers regular ferry services from the mainland to Koh Samui and is known for its reliability and comfortable journey.
- **Departure Points:**

- ◦ **Surat Thani (Donsak Pier):** A popular route, taking about 1.5 hours to reach Koh Samui.
  - ◦ **Nakhon Si Thammarat:** Provides additional options for travelers coming from southern Thailand.
- **Facilities:** Onboard facilities typically include seating areas, restrooms, and a snack bar.

2. Lomprayah High-Speed Ferries

- **Overview:** Lomprayah operates high-speed catamarans, which are faster than conventional ferries and provide a smooth ride to Koh Samui.
- **Departure Points:**
  - ◦ **Surat Thani (Donsak Pier):** Approximately 1.5 hours to Koh Samui.
  - ◦ **Koh Tao and Koh Phangan:** Lomprayah also connects these nearby islands, making it easy to island-hop.
- **Facilities:** Passengers can enjoy comfortable seating, refreshments, and air-conditioning on the high-speed vessels.

3. Ferry Schedules and Tickets

- **Booking:** Tickets for ferries can be purchased at the terminal or booked online in advance for

convenience, especially during peak travel seasons.
- **Travel Tips:** It's advisable to check the ferry schedules in advance as they can vary depending on the season and weather conditions. Travelers should aim to arrive at least 30 minutes prior to departure for check-in.

Getting to Koh Samui is convenient, thanks to the availability of both air and ferry services. Whether you prefer a direct flight to Samui International Airport or a scenic ferry ride from the mainland, there are multiple options to suit every traveler's preference. With a little planning, you can easily embark on your adventure to this tropical paradise.

Transportation Within Koh Samui

Getting around Koh Samui is relatively easy and offers a variety of options, from public transportation to rental services. Whether you prefer the convenience of a private vehicle or the local charm of public transport, there are multiple ways to explore the island and its stunning attractions.

Public Transportation

Songthaews

Songthaews are the most popular and economical way to travel around Koh Samui. These shared pickup trucks operate as a form of public transport and can be seen throughout the island.

- **Overview:** Songthaews typically have two rows of seating in the back and run on set routes, making them an excellent option for tourists who want to explore local attractions without breaking the bank.
- **Cost:** Fares are affordable, usually ranging from 20 to 100 THB, depending on the distance traveled.
- **How to Use:** You can catch a songthaew at designated stops or wave one down on the street. Let the driver know your destination, and pay once you reach it.
- **Tips:** It's a good idea to confirm the fare before starting your journey, especially for longer distances.

Taxis

While taxis are available on the island, they operate differently than in many cities worldwide.

- **Overview:** Koh Samui taxis are usually not metered, and fares should be negotiated before the ride. Drivers typically display their prices on a board in the vehicle.
- **Cost:** Taxi fares vary based on distance and time of day. Expect to pay between 200 and 1,000 THB for popular destinations.
- **Booking:** You can find taxis at major tourist areas, hotels, and the airport. It's advisable to book in advance through your hotel or a local travel agency for convenience.

Renting a Car or Motorbike

For those who prefer more independence and flexibility in their travel plans, renting a car or motorbike is a great option.

Renting a Motorbike

- **Overview:** Renting a motorbike is one of the most popular ways to explore Koh Samui. It offers the freedom to visit various attractions at your own pace.

- **Requirements:** You'll need a valid motorcycle license and an international driving permit to rent a motorbike legally.
- **Cost:** Daily rental prices typically range from 150 to 500 THB, depending on the bike's model and rental duration.
- **Tips:** Always inspect the bike for any damages before renting and take photos as proof. Helmets are mandatory, and wearing one is crucial for safety.

Renting a Car

- **Overview:** Renting a car is another option, especially for families or groups. It provides comfort and shelter from the tropical sun.
- **Requirements:** A valid driver's license and an international driving permit are required.
- **Cost:** Daily car rental prices start from around 1,000 THB and can go up depending on the vehicle type and rental duration.
- **Tips:** Be mindful of local driving laws, as traffic can be chaotic, and some roads may be poorly maintained. Always check the fuel policy before renting.

Bicycle Rentals

Bicycles are a sustainable and enjoyable way to explore Koh Samui, particularly in less crowded areas.

- **Overview:** Many shops across the island offer bicycle rentals, making it easy to navigate through quieter neighborhoods and beaches.
- **Cost:** Daily rental fees for bicycles generally range from 100 to 300 THB, depending on the bike type and rental shop.
- **Best Areas for Cycling:** Consider exploring areas like the serene coastline of Taling Ngam or the lush surroundings near Maenam.
- **Tips:** Always wear a helmet and follow local traffic rules. Carry water and sunscreen, especially if you plan on cycling for extended periods.

Driving Tips and Safety Regulations in Koh Samui

Driving in Koh Samui can be an exciting way to explore the island at your own pace, but it is essential to familiarize yourself with local driving regulations and conditions to ensure a safe and enjoyable experience. Here are some vital tips and guidelines for foreign drivers navigating the island's roads.

Rules for Foreign Drivers

1. Driving License Requirements

Foreigners wishing to drive in Koh Samui must possess a valid driver's license from their home country along with an International Driving Permit (IDP). The IDP is crucial as it translates your license into multiple languages, making it easier for local authorities to understand.

2. Vehicle Insurance

Ensure that you have valid insurance coverage for the vehicle you are renting. Most rental companies provide basic insurance, but it is wise to confirm coverage for theft, damage, and liability.

3. Traffic Laws

- **Driving Side:** In Thailand, vehicles drive on the left side of the road. Be aware of this before starting your journey.
- **Speed Limits:** Speed limits are generally 60 km/h in urban areas, 80 km/h on rural roads, and up to 90 km/h on highways. Always obey posted signs.
- **Seat Belts:** Seat belts are mandatory for all passengers. Ensure that everyone in the vehicle is buckled up before driving.
- **Mobile Phone Use:** Using a mobile phone while driving is prohibited unless you have a hands-free device.

4. Alcohol Consumption

The legal blood alcohol limit in Thailand is 0.05%. It is highly advisable to avoid drinking and driving altogether, as penalties for violations can be severe, including fines, license suspension, or imprisonment.

Navigating the Island's Roads

1. Road Conditions

The quality of roads in Koh Samui can vary significantly. While main roads connecting major tourist areas and attractions are generally well-maintained, some smaller roads may be narrow, bumpy, or have potholes. Exercise caution and drive slowly in such areas.

2. Traffic Congestion
Koh Samui can experience heavy traffic, particularly during peak tourist seasons and rush hours. Allow extra time for travel and consider avoiding busy routes during these periods. Use local maps or navigation apps to plan your routes effectively.

3. Roundabouts and Intersections
Roundabouts are common in Koh Samui. Vehicles inside the roundabout have the right of way, so yield to them when approaching. At intersections without traffic lights, be cautious and yield to oncoming traffic.

4. Wildlife and Animals
Keep an eye out for animals, such as dogs, cows, and monkeys, which may roam freely along the roads. Be prepared to stop suddenly if an animal crosses your path.

5. Parking
Parking is generally available near tourist attractions and shopping areas, but it may be limited in busy areas. Ensure you park in designated spaces and avoid blocking driveways or entrances. Be cautious of local parking regulations to avoid fines.

Driving in Koh Samui can enhance your travel experience, allowing you to explore the island's hidden gems and beautiful landscapes. However, understanding and adhering to local driving regulations and safety tips is crucial for a safe journey. By following these guidelines, you can enjoy the freedom of driving while ensuring a memorable and trouble-free adventure on this stunning island.

Car Rental Companies and Contact Information in Koh Samui

Renting a car in Koh Samui is an excellent way to explore the island's beautiful landscapes, hidden beaches, and vibrant local culture. Several reputable car rental companies offer various vehicles to suit your needs, from compact cars to larger SUVs. Here's a list of popular car rental companies in Koh Samui, along with their contact information and key details.

Popular Car Rental Companies

1. Samui Car Rent

- **Overview:** Offers a wide range of vehicles, including economy cars, SUVs, and luxury options. The company is known for its excellent customer service and transparent pricing.
- **Contact Information:**
    - **Website:** [Samui Car Rent](#)
    - **Phone:** +66 77 424 255
    - **Email:** info@samuicarrent.com
- **Location:** Conveniently located near Samui Airport, making it easy to pick up a vehicle upon arrival.

2. Koh Samui Car Rental

- **Overview:** Provides a variety of vehicles, including motorcycles, scooters, and cars. They offer flexible rental terms and delivery services to your accommodation.
- **Contact Information:**
    - **Website:** [Koh Samui Car Rental](#)
    - **Phone:** +66 77 430 601
    - **Email:** info@kohsamui-carrental.com
- **Location:** Various locations around the island, including airport pickup.

3. Sixt Rent a Car

- **Overview:** A well-known international rental company offering a range of vehicles, including luxury and high-end options. They are recognized for their professional service and extensive fleet.
- **Contact Information:**
    - **Website:** [Sixt Koh Samui](#)
    - **Phone:** +66 77 429 998
- **Location:** Located at Samui Airport and in several spots across the island.

4. Budget Car Rental

- **Overview:** Part of a reputable global brand, Budget Car Rental offers competitive rates on a variety of vehicles. They provide both short-term and long-term rentals.
- **Contact Information:**
    - **Website:** [Budget Thailand](#)
    - **Phone:** +66 77 420 919
- **Location:** Available at Samui Airport and selected hotels on the island.

5. Thai Rent A Car

- **Overview:** Offers a diverse selection of vehicles, including compact cars, minivans, and pickup

trucks. They have a solid reputation for reliability and customer service.
- **Contact Information:**
  - **Website:** Thai Rent A Car
  - **Phone:** +66 77 429 200
- **Location:** Located near the airport and in various locations throughout Koh Samui.

Directions to Tourist Centers and Attractions

Once you've rented your car, you'll want to explore the many attractions Koh Samui has to offer. Below are directions to some popular tourist centers and attractions on the island, making it easier for you to navigate your way around.

1. Big Buddha Temple (Wat Phra Yai)

- **Address:** 99/9 Moo 4, Bophut, Koh Samui, Surat Thani 84320, Thailand
- **Directions:** From Chaweng Beach, head north along Route 4171. Follow the signs to Bophut and turn left onto the road leading to the temple. The Big Buddha is easily visible from the road, and parking is available nearby.

2. Ang Thong National Marine Park

- **Address:** Ang Thong National Marine Park, Koh Samui, Surat Thani 84140, Thailand
- **Directions:** To reach the park, drive to Nathon Pier, located on the western side of the island. From there, you can catch a boat tour to the marine park. Follow Route 4170 to Nathon and look for signs to the pier.

3. Namuang Waterfalls

- **Address:** Namuang Waterfall 1, Na Mueang, Koh Samui, Surat Thani 84140, Thailand
- **Directions:** From Chaweng, take Route 4169 south towards Namuang. Follow the signs to Namuang Waterfalls. The waterfalls are located about 15 minutes from Chaweng, with parking available at the entrance.

4. Wat Plai Laem

- **Address:** 33 Moo 5, Bophut, Koh Samui, Surat Thani 84320, Thailand
- **Directions:** Drive along Route 4171 from Chaweng towards Bophut. Look for signs directing you to Wat Plai Laem. The temple is just off the main road, with parking available on-site.

5. Hin Ta and Hin Yai Rocks (Grandfather and Grandmother Rocks)

- **Address:** 3/1 Moo 3, Lamai, Koh Samui, Surat Thani 84310, Thailand
- **Directions:** Head south on Route 4169 from Chaweng toward Lamai Beach. Follow the signs to Hin Ta and Hin Yai Rocks, which are located near Lamai Beach. There is a parking area close to the rocks.

Renting a car in Koh Samui provides the flexibility to explore the island's stunning attractions at your own pace. With various reputable rental companies and clear directions to key tourist centers, you can enjoy a smooth and enjoyable driving experience. Always remember to check local traffic rules, drive safely, and take in the beautiful scenery along the way.

CHAPTER SEVEN

Sample Itineraries, Customs, and Traditions

Sample Itineraries for Different Types of Travelers in Koh Samui

Koh Samui is a versatile destination, catering to a variety of traveler interests, whether it's adventure, relaxation, or cultural exploration. Below are sample itineraries designed for different types of travelers, providing an organized plan for experiencing the island in a way that aligns with their preferences.

3-Day Itinerary for First-Time Visitors

Day 1: Arrival and Beach Exploration

- **Morning:** Arrive at Koh Samui Airport and pick up your rental car. Check into your hotel.
- **Afternoon:** Head to **Chaweng Beach** for a leisurely afternoon. Enjoy swimming, sunbathing, or trying out water sports like jet skiing or parasailing.

- **Evening:** Dinner at **Prego Italian Restaurant** in Chaweng, known for its authentic Italian cuisine and beach views.

Day 2: Cultural Highlights

- **Morning:** Visit **Big Buddha Temple (Wat Phra Yai)**. Take some time to explore the temple grounds and enjoy the stunning views.
- **Afternoon:** Head to **Wat Plai Laem**, a beautiful temple complex with impressive statues. Spend some time enjoying the tranquil atmosphere.
- **Evening:** Explore the vibrant **Fisherman's Village in Bophut**. Stroll along the beach, shop at local boutiques, and have dinner at **Coco Tam's**, famous for its beachside dining.

Day 3: Nature and Adventure

- **Morning:** Take a half-day tour to **Ang Thong National Marine Park** for snorkeling and kayaking in crystal-clear waters.
- **Afternoon:** Return to Koh Samui and relax at **Lamai Beach**, soaking in the sun.
- **Evening:** Enjoy a farewell dinner at **Dining on the Rocks** for a memorable culinary experience with panoramic views.

5-Day Adventure Itinerary

Day 1: Arrival and Beach Relaxation

- **Morning:** Arrive in Koh Samui and check into your hotel.
- **Afternoon:** Spend time at **Silver Beach (Haad Thongtakian)**, enjoying its tranquility and stunning scenery.
- **Evening:** Dinner at **The Cliff Bar & Grill**, overlooking the ocean.

Day 2: Waterfall and Jungle Safari

- **Morning:** Visit **Namuang Waterfalls** for a refreshing swim. Hike to the second waterfall if you're feeling adventurous.
- **Afternoon:** Join an **Off-Road Jungle Safari** tour. Explore hidden spots and enjoy the lush landscapes of Koh Samui.
- **Evening:** Relax and have dinner at a local restaurant.

Day 3: Marine Adventure

- **All Day:** Take a day trip to **Ang Thong National Marine Park**. Snorkel, kayak, and hike to viewpoints for breathtaking views of the islands.

- **Evening:** Return to Koh Samui and enjoy a casual dinner at **Lamai Night Market**, sampling local street food.

Day 4: Zip-Lining and Island Hopping

- **Morning:** Experience **zip-lining** through the jungle canopy. Companies like **Canopy Adventures** offer thrilling courses with stunning views.
- **Afternoon:** Relax at **Taling Ngam Beach** or take a short boat trip to **Koh Taen** (Coral Island) for snorkeling and beach time.
- **Evening:** Dine at **The Boudoir**, known for its intimate setting and exquisite food.

Day 5: Departure

- **Morning:** Last-minute shopping at local markets or relaxation at the beach.
- **Afternoon:** Check out from your hotel and head to the airport for your departure.

Relaxation-Focused Itinerary

Day 1: Arrival and Spa Day

- **Morning:** Arrive in Koh Samui and check into a beachfront resort.
- **Afternoon:** Unwind with a spa treatment at the hotel or a nearby wellness center, like **Tamarind Springs Forest Spa**.
- **Evening:** Dinner at **Zazen Restaurant**, known for its peaceful atmosphere and fine dining.

Day 2: Leisurely Beach Day

- **Morning:** Enjoy breakfast with a view. Then, relax at **Lipa Noi Beach**, famous for its soft sands and gentle waves.
- **Afternoon:** Take a leisurely walk along the beach or enjoy a book by the shore.
- **Evening:** Casual dining at **The Fisherman's Village** in Bophut. Enjoy local cuisine at **Barracuda Restaurant**.

Day 3: Yoga and Cultural Exploration

- **Morning:** Participate in a **yoga class** at a local studio, such as **Samahita Retreat**.
- **Afternoon:** Visit **Wat Plai Laem** for a peaceful afternoon of exploration and photography.

- **Evening:** Dinner at **Coco Tam's**, enjoying the sunset over the water.

Day 4: Nature and Scenic Views

- **Morning:** Take a trip to **Secret Buddha Garden**. Explore the lush landscape and serene statues.
- **Afternoon:** Head to **Namuang Waterfalls** for a relaxing swim in the natural pools.
- **Evening:** Dine at **Dining on the Rocks**, a fine dining restaurant with spectacular views of the Gulf of Thailand.

Day 5: Departure

- **Morning:** Enjoy a leisurely breakfast and a final stroll along the beach.
- **Afternoon:** Check out and head to the airport for your departure.

These itineraries provide a structured yet flexible way to enjoy Koh Samui, catering to different traveler types and ensuring a memorable experience on this stunning island.

Dos and Don'ts for Respectful Travel in Koh Samui

Traveling to Koh Samui can be an enriching experience, but respecting the local culture and customs is essential to ensure a positive interaction with the island's residents and its environment. Here are some practical dos and don'ts to help you navigate your journey in a respectful manner.

Dos

1. Do Dress Appropriately
When visiting temples and religious sites, dress modestly. Wear clothing that covers your shoulders and knees, and remove your shoes before entering sacred areas.

2. Do Respect Local Customs
Be aware of local traditions and practices. For example, it is customary to greet locals with a slight bow of the head and a smile rather than a handshake.

3. Do Participate in Local Festivals
Engage in local festivals and cultural celebrations if possible. These events provide a wonderful opportunity to experience Thai culture and interact with locals.

4. Do Use Polite Language

While English is commonly spoken in tourist areas, learning a few basic Thai phrases can be greatly appreciated. Simple greetings like "Sawasdee" (hello) and "Khop Khun" (thank you) can go a long way.

5. Do Be Mindful of the Environment

Koh Samui's natural beauty is one of its biggest attractions. Be sure to respect the environment by not littering, avoiding single-use plastics, and participating in beach clean-ups if you come across one.

6. Do Bargain Respectfully

If shopping at markets, bargaining is common. However, do so respectfully and with a smile. It's important to maintain a friendly attitude while negotiating prices.

7. Do Respect Religious Practices

If you witness locals engaged in religious practices or ceremonies, observe quietly from a distance. Avoid interrupting or taking photographs unless you have permission.

Don'ts

1. Don't Disrespect the Royal Family
Thailand has strict laws regarding the monarchy, and disrespecting the royal family is taken very seriously. Avoid making negative comments or jokes about the King or royal family members.

2. Don't Touch Heads
In Thai culture, the head is considered the most sacred part of the body. Avoid touching someone's head, even if it's a child's, as this is seen as disrespectful.

3. Don't Display Public Affection
While holding hands is generally acceptable, more intimate displays of affection such as kissing or hugging in public may be frowned upon, especially in more traditional areas.

4. Don't Use Your Feet to Point or Touch
Feet are considered the dirtiest part of the body in Thai culture. Avoid pointing with your feet or using them to touch objects or people. If you need to show someone something, use your hand instead.

5. Don't Engage in Arguments
Thais value politeness and composure. Avoid raising your voice or engaging in arguments, especially in

public. If a situation becomes tense, remain calm and polite.

6. Don't Ignore Local Advice

When engaging in outdoor activities or visiting natural attractions, listen to local advice and follow any posted guidelines. This not only ensures your safety but also helps preserve the environment.

7. Don't Litter or Damage Nature

Koh Samui is known for its stunning landscapes and beaches. Help preserve the natural beauty by not littering and being cautious not to damage coral reefs or marine life when snorkeling or diving.

By following these dos and don'ts, travelers can show respect for the local culture and traditions of Koh Samui. This respectful approach will not only enhance your travel experience but also foster positive interactions with the island's residents, making your visit memorable for all the right reasons.

Useful Phrases in Thai

Learning a few basic phrases in Thai can greatly enhance your travel experience in Koh Samui and help you connect with the locals. Here's a list of useful phrases along with their English translations, pronunciation tips, and contexts in which you might use them.

Basic Greetings

- **Hello**
  Thai: สวัสดี (Sawasdee)
  Usage: A general greeting at any time of day.
  Pronunciation: sah-wah-dee
- **Goodbye**
  Thai: ลาก่อน (Laa-gorn)
  Usage: Used when parting ways.
  Pronunciation: lah-gawn
- **How are you?**
  Thai: สบายดีไหม? (Sabai dee mai?)
  Usage: Used to ask someone how they are.
  Pronunciation: sah-bai dee mai?

Polite Expressions

- **Thank you**
  Thai: ขอบคุณ (Khop khun)

- **Usage:** Used to express gratitude.
    Pronunciation: kop-koon
  - **You're welcome**
    Thai: ยินดี (Yindi)
    Usage: Used in response to "thank you."
    Pronunciation: yin-dee
  - **Please**
    Thai: กรุณา (Karuna)
    Usage: Used when making requests.
    Pronunciation: ka-roo-na

Common Questions

  - **Where is...?**
    Thai: ...อยู่ที่ไหน? (...yuu tee nai?)
    Usage: Use this to ask for directions.
    Pronunciation: ...yoo tee nai?
  - **How much is this?**
    Thai: อันนี้ราคาเท่าไหร่? (An nee ra-kha thao-rai?)
    Usage: Useful when shopping.
    Pronunciation: an nee rah-kah tao-rai?
  - **Do you speak English?**
    Thai: คุณพูดภาษาอังกฤษได้ไหม? (Khun pood pa-sa ang-grit dai mai?)
    Usage: A helpful phrase when you need assistance in English.
    Pronunciation: khun poot pah-sah ang-grit dai mai?

Dining and Shopping

- **Delicious**
  Thai: อร่อย (Aroi)
  Usage: To compliment the food.
  Pronunciation: ah-roy
- **I would like...**
  Thai: ฉันต้องการ... (Chan tong karn...)
  Usage: Use this when ordering food or requesting items.
  Pronunciation: chan tong-gahn...
- **Check, please**
  Thai: ขอเช็คบิลด้วย (Kho chek bin duay)
  Usage: Used to ask for the bill at restaurants.
  Pronunciation: kho chek bin duay

Transportation

- **Where is the bus station?**
  Thai: สถานีรถบัสอยู่ที่ไหน? (Sa-tha-nee rot bus yuu tee nai?)
  Usage: Helpful when looking for transport options.
  Pronunciation: sa-tha-nee rot bus yoo tee nai?
- **I want to go to...**
  Thai: ฉันอยากไป... (Chan yahk bpai...)
  Usage: Use when telling a taxi driver your

destination.
Pronunciation: chan yahk bpai...

Emergency Phrases

- **Help!**
  Thai: ช่วยด้วย! (Chuay duay!)
  Usage: Used in emergencies.
  Pronunciation: chua-y duay
- **I need a doctor**
  Thai: ฉันต้องการหมอ (Chan tong karn mor)
  Usage: Important to know in case of medical emergencies.
  Pronunciation: chan tong-garn mor
- **Call the police!**
  Thai: โทรหาตำรวจ (Tor haa tam-ruat)
  Usage: In case you need police assistance.
  Pronunciation: tor haa tam-ruat

Using these phrases during your visit to Koh Samui can help break down barriers and foster a friendly atmosphere with the locals. Thai people generally appreciate any effort to speak their language, even if it's just a few words. Enjoy your journey!

Appendix

The appendix section of the Koh Samui Travel Guide provides crucial information that will aid travelers during their visit. It includes emergency contact numbers and details on bank locations and ATMs to ensure visitors have access to assistance and financial services when needed.

A.1 Emergency Contact Numbers

In case of emergencies, it's important to have quick access to relevant contact numbers. Below are key emergency contacts for Koh Samui:

- **Police:** 191
  For reporting crimes or emergencies requiring police intervention.
- **Ambulance and Medical Emergencies:** 1669
  For urgent medical assistance and ambulance services.
- **Fire Department:** 199
  For reporting fires or fire-related emergencies.
- **Tourist Police:** 1155
  Specifically for tourists, offering assistance in English and other languages.
- **Local Hospitals:**
  - **Samui International Hospital**
    Address: 27/9 Moo 3, Chaweng Beach

Road, Koh Samui, Surat Thani 84320
Phone: +66 77 414 055
Services include emergency care, general medicine, and specialized treatments.
- **Bangkok Samui Hospital**
  Address: 99/1 Moo 2, Koh Samui, Surat Thani 84140
  Phone: +66 77 960 888
  This private hospital offers comprehensive medical services and facilities.

A.2 Bank Locations and ATMs

Koh Samui offers a variety of banking options and ATMs, ensuring visitors have access to their funds. Here's a list of banks and their ATM locations:

- **Bangkok Bank**
  Address: 165/1 Moo 2, Chaweng Beach, Koh Samui, Surat Thani 84320
  Services: Provides a range of banking services, including currency exchange and wire transfers.
  ATM Locations: Available at the bank branch and other locations around Chaweng.
- **Kasikorn Bank**
  Address: 97/13 Moo 1, Bophut, Koh Samui,

Surat Thani 84320

Services: Offers personal banking, loans, and investment services.

ATM Locations: Multiple ATMs are scattered throughout the island.

- **Siam Commercial Bank (SCB)**
Address: 162/15 Moo 2, Chaweng, Koh Samui, Surat Thani 84320

Services: Comprehensive banking services including loans and insurance products.

ATM Locations: ATMs are located in the vicinity of the bank branch and major shopping areas.

- **Thai Military Bank (TMB)**
Address: 59/1 Moo 4, Maenam, Koh Samui, Surat Thani 84330

Services: Provides retail banking services and personal loans.

ATM Locations: ATMs can be found near tourist attractions and shopping centers.

- **Currency Exchange**
Various currency exchange booths and services are available at the airport, major tourist areas, and markets, providing competitive rates for exchanging currency.

A.3 Recommended Travel Apps for Koh Samui

To make the most of your trip to Koh Samui, consider downloading the following travel apps that provide useful information and services:

- **Google Maps**
  An essential app for navigation, Google Maps offers detailed maps of Koh Samui, including walking, driving, and public transport directions. You can also find nearby attractions, restaurants, and points of interest.
- **Grab**
  This popular ride-hailing app is widely used in Southeast Asia. Grab provides safe and convenient transportation options, including taxis and motorbike taxis, making it easier to get around the island.
- **Koh Samui Map**
  A specialized map app for Koh Samui, it provides offline maps and detailed information about local attractions, restaurants, and accommodations, helping you navigate without needing an internet connection.
- **TripAdvisor**
  This app allows you to explore reviews, ratings, and recommendations for attractions, restaurants,

and activities in Koh Samui. You can also find travel itineraries and book experiences directly through the app.
- **Language Translation Apps (e.g., Google Translate)**

  A translation app can be extremely helpful for communicating with locals, especially in areas where English is not widely spoken. You can use it for text translation and even voice input for conversations.
- **Weather Apps (e.g., AccuWeather, Weather Underground)**

  Stay informed about the weather conditions in Koh Samui with reliable weather apps. These apps provide forecasts, current weather updates, and alerts for any weather changes that may impact your travel plans.
- **Local SIM Card Providers (e.g., AIS, TrueMove)**

  If you plan to stay connected while in Koh Samui, download apps from local telecom providers to manage your prepaid SIM card, check data usage, and recharge your plan easily.

A.4 Tourist Information Centers and Contact Details

Tourist information centers are valuable resources for travelers seeking assistance, local tips, and maps. Here are some key tourist information centers in Koh Samui:

- **Koh Samui Tourist Information Center**
  Address: 35/3 Moo 3, Chaweng Beach Road, Bophut, Koh Samui, Surat Thani 84320
  Phone: +66 77 422 106
  Hours: Daily, 9:00 AM - 5:00 PM
  Services: Provides maps, brochures, and general information about attractions, activities, transportation, and accommodation. Staffed by knowledgeable locals who can assist with recommendations.

- **Bophut Tourist Information Center**
  Address: Fisherman's Village, Bophut Beach, Koh Samui, Surat Thani 84320
  Phone: +66 77 430 088
  Hours: Daily, 10:00 AM - 4:00 PM
  Services: Offers tourist information specific to the Bophut area, including local events, dining options, and activities. You can also find guided tour information here.

- **Nathon Tourist Information Center**
  Address: Nathon Beach, Koh Samui, Surat Thani 84140
  Phone: +66 77 421 133
  Hours: Daily, 9:00 AM - 5:00 PM
  Services: Focused on providing information for those arriving by ferry and exploring the west side of the island. It offers maps, transportation options, and recommendations for local attractions.
- **Lamai Tourist Information Center**
  Address: Near Lamai Beach, Koh Samui, Surat Thani 84310
  Phone: +66 77 233 567
  Hours: Daily, 9:00 AM - 5:00 PM
  Services: Provides information on Lamai Beach activities, dining options, and cultural events in the area. A great resource for local insights and tips.

CONCLUSION

Koh Samui Travel Guide 2025 serves as your comprehensive companion, ensuring that every aspect of your trip is not only memorable but also well-planned and stress-free. From the sun-kissed beaches of Chaweng and Lamai to the tranquil secret spots like the Magic Garden and Overlap Stone, Koh Samui is a tropical paradise brimming with adventure, relaxation, and cultural immersion. The island's diverse offerings cater to every type of traveler—whether you're a first-time visitor seeking the island's highlights, an adventure enthusiast eager for off-road safaris and marine exploration, or someone looking for peaceful solitude along its lesser-known shores.

With essential travel information, local customs, and detailed recommendations on accommodation, dining, and transportation, this guide equips you with everything you need to know before stepping foot on the island. Beyond the practicalities, it inspires a deeper connection with Koh Samui's rich history, vibrant culture, and natural beauty, offering a gateway to experiences that go beyond the ordinary tourist paths.

As you embark on your journey, let this guide help you navigate the wonders of Koh Samui, making your stay not just a vacation, but an adventure filled with discoveries, from bustling street markets and world-class cuisine to hidden gems and quiet sanctuaries. Whether you're drawn to its stunning beaches, cultural landmarks, or thrilling outdoor pursuits, Koh Samui offers a travel experience that will leave you captivated, enriched, and yearning to return.

Enjoy the magic of Koh Samui, and let this guide be your trusted roadmap to an unforgettable island getaway.

TRAVEL

DATE:
DURATION:

DESTINATION:

PLACES TO SEE:	LOCAL FOOD TO TRY:
1	1
2	2
3	3
4	4
5	5
6	6
7	7

DAY 1	DAY 2	DAY 3

DAY 4	DAY 5	DAY 6

NOTES	EXPENSES IN TOTAL:

PLANNER

TRAVEL

DATE:
DURATION:

DESTINATION:

PLACES TO SEE:	LOCAL FOOD TO TRY:
1	1
2	2
3	3
4	4
5	5
6	6
7	7

DAY 1	DAY 2	DAY 3

DAY 4	DAY 5	DAY 6

NOTES	EXPENSES IN TOTAL:

PLANNER

TRAVEL

DATE:
DURATION:

DESTINATION:

PLACES TO SEE:
1. ___
2. ___
3. ___
4. ___
5. ___
6. ___
7. ___

LOCAL FOOD TO TRY:
1. ___
2. ___
3. ___
4. ___
5. ___
6. ___
7. ___

DAY 1	DAY 2	DAY 3

DAY 4	DAY 5	DAY 6

NOTES

EXPENSES IN TOTAL:

PLANNER

TRAVEL PLANNER

DATE:
DURATION:
DESTINATION:

PLACES TO SEE:
1. ___
2. ___
3. ___
4. ___
5. ___
6. ___
7. ___

LOCAL FOOD TO TRY:
1. ___
2. ___
3. ___
4. ___
5. ___
6. ___
7. ___

DAY 1	DAY 2	DAY 3

DAY 4	DAY 5	DAY 6

NOTES

EXPENSES IN TOTAL:

TRAVEL PLANNER

DATE:
DURATION:
DESTINATION:

PLACES TO SEE:
1.
2.
3.
4.
5.
6.
7.

LOCAL FOOD TO TRY:
1.
2.
3.
4.
5.
6.
7.

DAY 1	DAY 2	DAY 3

DAY 4	DAY 5	DAY 6

NOTES

EXPENSES IN TOTAL:

TRAVEL

DATE:
DURATION:

DESTINATION:

PLACES TO SEE:
1. _____
2. _____
3. _____
4. _____
5. _____
6. _____
7. _____

LOCAL FOOD TO TRY:
1. _____
2. _____
3. _____
4. _____
5. _____
6. _____
7. _____

DAY 1	DAY 2	DAY 3

DAY 4	DAY 5	DAY 6

NOTES

EXPENSES IN TOTAL:

PLANNER

Printed in Great Britain
by Amazon